bs.

Tourism in Peripheral Areas

ASPECTS OF TOURISM

Series Editors:
Professor Chris Cooper, *University of Queensland, Ipswich, Australia*
Dr Michael Hall, *University of Otago, Dunedin, New Zealand.*
Professor Alastair Morrison, *Purdue University, Lafayette, USA*

Aspects of Tourism is an innovative, multifaceted series which will comprise authoritative reference handbooks on global tourism regions, research volumes, texts and monographs. It is designed to provide readers with the latest thinking on tourism worldwide and in so doing will push back the frontiers of tourism knowledge. The series will also introduce a new generation of international tourism authors writing on leading-edge topics.

The volumes will be authoritative, readable and user-friendly, providing accessible sources for further research. The list will be underpinned by an annual authoritative tourism research volume. Books in the series will be commissioned probing the relationship between tourism and cognate subject areas such as strategy, development, retailing, sport and environmental studies. The publisher and series editors welcome proposals from writers with projects on these topics.

Other Books in the Series
Dynamic Tourism
    Priscilla Boniface
Journeys into Otherness: The Representation of Differences and Identity in Tourism
    Keith Hollinshead and Chuck Burlo (eds)
Tourism Collaboration and Partnerships
    Bill Bramwell and Bernard Lane (eds)
Tourism and Development: Concepts and Issues
    Richard Sharpley and David Telfer (eds)

Please contact us for the latest book information:
Channel View Publications, Frankfurt Lodge, Clevedon Hall,
Victoria Road, Clevedon, BS21 7HH, England
http://www.multilingual-matters.com

ASPECTS OF TOURISM 2
Series Editors:
Chris Cooper, *University of Queensland, Australia*
Michael Hall, *University of Otago, New Zealand*
Alastair Morrison, *Purdue University, USA*

Tourism in Peripheral Areas

Case Studies

Edited by
Frances Brown and Derek Hall

CHANNEL VIEW PUBLICATIONS
Clevedon • Buffalo • Toronto • Sydney

Library of Congress Cataloging in Publication Data

Tourism in Peripheral Areas: Case Studies/Edited by Frances Brown and Derek Hall
Aspects of Tourism: 2
Includes bibliographical references
1. Tourism–Europe–Case studies. 2. Rural development–Case studies.
I. Brown, Frances. II. Hall, Derek. III. Series.
G155.E8 T678 2000
338.4'791404–dc21   00-031456

British Library Cataloguing in Publication Data

A CIP catalogue record for this book is available from the British Library.

ISBN 1-853150-23-7 (hbk)

Channel View Publications
An imprint of Multilingual Matters Ltd

UK: Frankfurt Lodge, Clevedon Hall, Victoria Road, Clevedon BS21 7SJ.
USA: 2250 Military Road, Tonawanda, NY 14150, USA.
Canada: 5201 Dufferin Street, North York, Ontario, Canada M3H 5T8.
Australia: P.O. Box 586, Artarmon, NSW, Australia.

Printed and bound in Great Britain by Cambrian Printers.

Contents

Preface

The impetus for this collection came from a conference on Peripheral Area Tourism organised by the Research Centre of Bornholm and held on the island in September 1997. The conference revealed a great and widespread interest in the subject matter and sparked a debate on the nature, meaning and practical consequences of tourism in the peripheral regions of Europe, of which these chapters are the result.

Some have been developed out of papers presented at the conference; others arose from research in progress being carried out by conference participants. All have been revised and brought up to date to reflect current thinking about – and experience of – tourism in a variety of locations on the periphery of Europe.

Introduction: The Paradox of Peripherality

FRANCES BROWN and DEREK HALL

The notion that most tourism activity takes place outside the world's main centres of production and population, in what Turner and Ash (1975) have termed *'the pleasure periphery'* – often assumed to comprise the countries of the developing world – is at the core of much writing on the subject. Nevertheless, there has been scant detailed research on tourism in countries or regions of countries deemed to be peripheral; this is particularly true for Europe, which is usually considered en bloc as a global core region.

Such a view of Europe is at best partial, however, and this volume aims to redress the balance by presenting a range of case studies on tourism in European peripheral areas and by exploring the paradox of threat and opportunity that this offers. For peripherality means different things to different people – one person's pristine wilderness is another's dismal wasteland – and its effects (see later) can be markedly different for long-time residents, incomers and tourists. Indeed, the aspirations of residents and visitors for the future development of peripheral areas may be seriously at odds. Whatever their feelings, however, we cannot discuss peripherality without some definition of what constitutes the phenomenon, and it is to this that we shall now turn.

What is Peripherality?

Peripherality has been defined as *'the outermost boundary of any area'* (Collins Concise Dictionary), a clearly spatial interpretation which can be applied without controversy to many of the places covered in this volume – the Orkney islands, the North Cape promontory at the tip of Norway, the sparsely populated wilderness of northern Sweden, for example.

But peripherality is more than merely a geographical notion. In modern parlance, to describe something as peripheral is often to dismiss it as unimportant, of no interest to the majority and of no significance to world events. In other words, to be peripheral is to be marginalised, to lack power and influence and it therefore carries social, political and economic implications. Thus it is that Wales, whose collapsed heavy industries no longer fuel the UK economy, and even part of the English county of Somerset, whose

1

unique wetland environment has little in common with 21st century urban living, must feel peripheral to the concerns of government decision-makers, while Northern Cyprus, part of an island that has been a hub of trade and tourism, has become an artificial periphery through political division, shunned by all the world's states except Turkey. It is this unequal or distant relationship with centres of power that marks out a periphery. For, as Scott points out in this volume, a periphery can only be a periphery in relation to some centre or core.

The idea of conceptualising the world as divided into core and periphery was a product of development studies and became part of dependency theory (see, e.g., Frank, 1967; Wallerstein, 1974). This posits an economic relationship between strong, industrialised countries or regions and weaker, agriculturally based states/regions often lacking an advanced technological infrastructure. In this relationship, the former are able to extract surplus from and impose unfair terms of trade on the latter, leading to their continuing economic disadvantage, which is often compounded by out-migration prompted by this same disadvantage.

In the tourism context, the concept has been applied (in a sweeping generalisation) to the relationship between the rich, industrialised tourist-generating countries and the less developed, often predominantly rural or coastal (especially small island) tourist-receiving regions. Here firms from the former remain in control of the industry and extract a holiday surplus from the latter, the profit from which these latter do not fully enjoy. In this case it is perhaps more useful to take Frank's (1967) notion of metropoles and satellites, rather than core and periphery, since it allows us to conceive of both satellite areas within the metropoles (e.g. the Somerset Levels in England) and metropoles in the satellites (e.g. Cardiff in Wales).

There are a number of problems both with dependency theory itself, which has failed to account either for the rise of formerly dependent states such as Singapore and Taiwan or for the growing interdependence of the (post)industrialised economies, and with its application to tourism, which cannot easily explain the vast numbers who visit metropolitan sites like Paris or Copenhagen, nor the fact that tourism development is often genuinely sought by many industrial areas now in decline as a vehicle for restructuring, and is not seen as exploitative. Nevertheless, several of the characteristics identified in dependency theory can be found in the countries and regions on the edge of Europe and these are summarised in Chapter 1 by Owen *et al.*

A peripheral area, then, is one that suffers from geographical isolation, being distant from core spheres of activity, with poor access to and from markets. It suffers also from economic marginalisation, caused either by an outright lack of resources or by a decline in traditional industries or agriculture, with much business activity in the hands of small micro-firms, which lack know-how and training in areas such as marketing and innovation, and are denied influence by dint of their fragmentation. There is a concomitant lack of infrastructure and a reliance on imports, leading to economic leakages; a largely rural setting where life has changed little in recent years; and a low and frequently declining or ageing population, which further exacerbates (or for some enhances) a sense of remoteness (Wanhill, 1997).

But beyond these objective characteristics, peripherality is also a matter of perception. A place that is remote and difficult to reach may be perceived by tourists (and others) to have certain qualities emblematic of its situation (natural beauty, quaintness, otherness) – qualities which are an attraction to some and a repellent to others. As Blomgren and Sørensen (1998: 334) have discussed, there is a mutual interdependence between these two sets of characteristics:

> the peripheral destination may possess symptoms of peripherality, but relies on the subjective interpretation of these symptoms by the tourist, while simultaneously the tourist will not perceive an area as peripheral without certain symbols of peripherality being present.

It is these perceptions which represent the key to the development of tourism in peripheral areas.

Paradox I

For, in general terms, as people in industrialised societies in the West react to the stresses of city life, and to long-term global shifts in production and consumption, with a seemingly insatiable interest in nature and the past (see Urry, 1990; 1995); and, in tourism terms, as tastes in holiday-taking have become more sophisticated and diverse, the attributes of peripherality, long viewed as disadvantageous, are now being seen as opportunities. Isolation and remoteness represent peace, difference, even exoticism. Rurality means nature – for mental contemplation, aesthetic appreciation or physical activity. Traditional lifestyles represent our heritage and the security of past times, while the fact that there is little scope for developing or attracting other industries makes tourism an attractive possibility for the maintenance or creation of jobs and the safeguarding of lifestyles, built heritage and environments. Paradoxically, it is the very symptoms of peripherality that now suggest an antidote to the economic and social problems it causes. Indeed, the European Union's Maastricht Treaty acknowledged in 1992 that tourism had a role to play in reducing regional disparities (Wanhill, 1997).

Paradox II

However, if the lure of remoteness and tradition proves too great or is not adequately managed, destinations that are beginning to prosper economically may become overcrowded, environmentally degraded or subject to pressure (both external and internal) to modernise and change, thereby losing the very characteristics that encouraged their success. In the case of North Cape, Jacobsen (Chapter 5) reports that, as well as attracting wilderness-seekers, the promontory is now regarded by some tourists as a site that '*should be seen*' – one to be ticked off – which has caused it to be regarded by yet others as '*too touristy*' and therefore to be avoided. Arel (Chapter 7) notes that holiday cottage construction in Sweden's Tärna mountains in the 1990s ignored vernacular styles and turned some resorts into Alpine clones.

Northern Cyprus, an unrecognised statelet since forcible partition of the island of Cyprus in 1974, presents a particularly interesting case. Despite attempts to attract non-Turkish tourists and investors, it remains perforce heavily dependent on Turkey because of its international pariah status. Its population is poor, with few economic opportunities, and many migrate to the Turkish mainland. Its doubly peripheral burden (depending on a country which is itself on the periphery of Europe) has meant, however, that its rich tourism resources have remained largely undeveloped (i.e. unspoilt) since 1974, particularly when compared with the Greek portion of the island or indeed with the southern Turkish coast. Its beaches are empty, its rich flora and fauna undisturbed, modern high-rise buildings are few and its Mediterranean way of life continues as it has done for years, albeit without its former Greek residents. In other words, it is a potential paradise (nay honeypot) for high-spending, eco- and culture tourists, who could provide the locals with the jobs, income and thus incentive to stay to maintain a viable community – but it is also currently complicated and relatively expensive to get to and most travel agents know little about it.

This would all change if a solution to the intractable Cyprus problem were found. Agents would be queuing up to do business in the north, with all the risks of concretisation, unplanned mass development and the sidelining of the local population that this could entail, not to mention the alienation of the very tourists to whom the destination currently appeals. Nor should we forget that the locals themselves might desire such development, in opposition to environmentalists, as was the case with the Akamas peninsula in the Greek Republic of Cyprus (Ioannides, 1995). Should a solution ever be reached, it will be interesting (or perhaps sobering) to see how far the north of the island is able to learn from the mistakes of other pleasure peripheries.

For the challenge is to develop tourism in Europe's peripheries in ways that will attract income and provide benefits to local residents while maintaining and, where possible, enhancing their uniqueness. Julie Scott's analysis of Northern Cyprus (Chapter 4) suggests a variety of outcomes for a case '*in waiting*' but there are already lessons to be drawn from the other cases presented in this volume – about tourists' perceptions of peripheral places and how these can be either modified or exploited, about involving the local community in tourism development (and the conflicts that may occur between different actors within that community), and about the economic and social value of using tourism not as a sole industry but as one element of diversification from other economies in retreat (Richards and Hall, 2000).

Thus David Botterill *et al.* (Chapter 1) present a series of mini-case studies examining how Wales' peripheral status and outsiders' perceptions of that status affect levels and types of tourism, as well as analysing causes of and public responses to the decline in certain products. Tourists' perceptions are also at the heart of Jens Jacobsen's chapter (4) on the North Cape, which finds that there are two quite distinct views of the promontory and discusses how it can be marketed to accommodate both of them. It also demonstrates that even the *'ultimate periphery'* may be considered too crowded by some.

In Chapter 2, a methodological study, Marcus Grant describes the Project Appraisal and Community Evaluation (PACE) process being piloted in the Somerset Levels. A mechanism designed to steer touristic and other land-use activities in a sustainable direction, taking account of social, economic and environmental impacts as well as of cumulative and inter-project effects, and capable of being used by all stakeholders, PACE could prove particularly suitable for fragile peripheral environments.

The environment of Orkney has always been its fortune but lately its high-quality and profitable farming industry has experienced difficulties, caused by changes in eating habits and a number of agricultural crises. In Chapter 5 Joy Gladstone and Angela Morris present findings of a survey of the diversification into tourism that has consequently taken place, with the offering of farm accommodation and the marketing of agricultural heritage as an attraction. All the businesses surveyed were micro-enterprises and the results build a picture of the constraints and opportunities facing these classic manifestations of development on the periphery. They also highlight respondents' assessment of the importance of support from the tourist authorities.

Bute, an island in the inner Hebrides, was once a thriving mass tourism resort much favoured as an escape from industrial Glasgow and well served by a veritable fleet of Clyde steamers. Today, however, with the decline in popularity of traditional British seaside holidays and the consequent withering of steamer services, Bute has arguably become more rather than less peripheral. Stephen Boyne *et al.* use Chapter 6 to analyse the reconfiguration of the island, now being targeted to visitors from England and overseas, who are being encouraged to view it as an exotic destination – positively peripheral – rather than one that is difficult to get to – negatively peripheral.

Finally, two Swedish chapters focus on tourism in the mountainous, forested north of that country. Nils Arel's history of tourism development in the Tärna mountains (Chapter 7) shows that tourism often has a longer pedigree than assumed, even in peripheral areas, but demonstrates the shifting roles played and influence wielded by different actors both within and outside the community over time. It is clear that external actors now play a more important role and, while this has helped open up the area, it has also erased some of its more distinctive features. Per Åke Nilsson (Chapter 8) continues this theme with examination of a project set up to try to increase jobs and turnover in tourism enterprises in the region of Arjeplog. The degree of endogenous and exogenous involvement in the firms studied is measured, as is the extent to which they are demand- or supply-side oriented. In this case it seems that experience from outside the community has been essential to the successful start-up of some of the firms in the study.

The cases presented in the following chapters all share certain similarities, but they also bear evidence of different approaches to tourism development, different solutions (or not) to its potential problems. Together they present much from which we can learn about the needs of peripheral areas and about how far and how best tourism can fulfil these needs, while reminding us that peripheries are not static phenomena destined never to change, even if some tourists would prefer that.

References

Blomgren, K.B. and Sørensen, A. (1998) Peripherality – factor or feature? Reflections on peripherality in tourism research. *Progress in Tourism and Hospitality Research* 4, 319–36.

Frank, A.G. (1967) *Capitalism and Underdevelopment in Latin America. Historical Studies of Chile and Brazil*. New York: Monthly Review Press.

Ioannides, D. (1995) A flawed implementation of sustainable tourism: The experience of Akamas, Cyprus. *Tourism Management* 16, 583–92.

Richards, G. and Hall, D. (eds) (2000) *Tourism and Sustainable Community Development*. London: Routledge.

Turner, L. and Ash, J. (1975) *The Golden Hordes*. London: Constable.

Urry, J. (1990) *The Tourist Gaze*. London: Sage.

Urry, J. (1995) *Consuming Places*. London: Routledge.

Wallerstein, E. (1974) *The Modern World-System: Capitalist Agriculture and the Origins of the European World-Economy in the Sixteenth Century*. New York: Academic Press.

Wanhill, S. (1997) Peripheral area tourism – a European perspective. *Progress in Tourism and Hospitality Research* 3, 47–70.

Chapter 1

Perceptions from the Periphery: The Experience of Wales

DAVID BOTTERILL, R. ELWYN OWEN, LOUISE EMANUEL, NICOLA
FOSTER, TIM GALE, CLIFF NELSON AND MARTIN SELBY

Introduction

This chapter looks critically at some of the key issues that underpin the notion of periphery, in the context of tourism in Wales. Ours is an excellent vantage point from which to examine issues regarding the periphery. Wales is a small country of some 2.8 million people, located on the western edge of Europe next to a larger neighbour. It bears many of the hallmarks of a peripheral area, having been traditionally regarded as one of the most economically disadvantaged parts of the United Kingdom. During the last two decades the economy of Wales has undergone a major transformation, with the old heavy industries of coal, iron and steel being replaced by a more diversified pattern of light manufacturing and service-based industries. Tourism is a major industry which, along with other elements of the economic and social fabric, has been subject to major structural change during recent years.

The chapter is in three parts. It begins with two introductory context-setting sections dealing respectively with the characteristics of peripheries and the main features of tourism in Wales. Two analytical themes set a framework for the consideration of five case studies in part three, which forms the paper's substantive core. Over the past five years several research projects have been in progress at the University of Wales Institute, Cardiff, examining different aspects of tourism in Wales. These studies provide recent empirical evidence of the condition of tourism in the periphery. Data from studies of place perception and rural tourism development, urban tourism, seaside holiday resorts, coastal pollution and international tourism to Wales are used to analyse critically tourism in the context of the core–periphery axiom.

The Periphery: Notions and Characteristics

Definitions

Humorists throughout the ages have warned us to choose our parents with care. Geographic humorists might remind us to choose our birthplaces with equal caution! Because it sums up so many economic and cultural considerations, our location in terms of nationality continues to be one of the prime determinants of our life – and indeed has a bearing on whether we will even survive the trauma of our birth. (Haggett, 1983)

This quotation highlights succinctly – possibly at the risk of trivialising – the fact that we live in an unequal world. These inequalities have long been the focus of academic interest, spawning a strong tradition of theoretical and empirical work under the banner of development and regional studies. They also raise challenging policy issues and have prompted a wide variety of official initiatives aimed at ameliorating economic and social imbalances at local, national and international levels.

Like any other specialist area, the field of development studies has its own terminology, which has evolved over time in response to new theoretical insights and fashion. Reflecting the subject matter itself, many of the terms have a hierarchical dimension: thus, they distinguish between rich and poor, developed and developing, north and south, and so on. The metaphors used to describe the status of an area within the development hierarchy have become more colourful over time and, on occasion, more abstruse. Thus, for example, a distinction has been drawn in the USA between rust belt and sun belt industries while in Europe the long established *'golden triangle'* has been joined by the *'blue banana'* regions (Brunet, 1989).

Two further and very potent terms within the development study lexicon are *'core'* and *'periphery'*. Their meaning can be encapsulated as follows:

In any geographical space – whether a nation, a group of nations (like western Europe) or the world, there is a tendency for inequalities to grow, because an advanced area or 'core' attracts resources that increase its leadership and thus its relative income. (Seers *et al.*, 1980)

Freedom of investment choice and the need to minimise transport costs has of course favoured the 'Golden triangle' countries in the EEC and operated to the disadvantage of peripheral industrial countries. (Kilby, 1980: 9)

Although the distinction between core and periphery is essentially a spatial one, the characteristics which set the two apart are often economic and social in nature. In brief, and at the risk of considerable over-simplification, the archetypal core location enjoys a high level of economic vitality, generally measured in terms of the value of the goods and services produced. It is metropolitan in character, and its residents enjoy a good standard of living and a vibrant lifestyle. The periphery, on the other hand, is characterised by relatively low levels of economic activity. Population is

sparser, reflecting the greater reliance on agriculture and allied rural industries. There is often a long tradition of out-migration to more favoured
areas. Infrastructure and social amenities tend to be poorer.

The nature of peripherality

It is beyond the scope of this paper to discuss in substantially more detail
the disparities between core and peripheral areas. It will be sufficient to
note that the literature identifies a number of salient characteristics which
set the two apart. The main ones are illustrated in Table 1.1 and then
described in more detail. They tend to be mutually reinforcing.

Table 1.1 Core and periphery: the key differences

	Core		*Periphery*
✓	High levels of economic vitality and a diverse economic base	✗	Low levels of economic vitality and dependent on traditional industries
✓	Metropolitan in character. Rising population through in-migration with a relatively young age structure	✗	More rural and remote – often with high scenic values. Population falling through out-migration, with an ageing structure
✓	Innovative, pioneering and enjoys good information flows	✗	Reliant on imported technologies and ideas, and suffers from poor information flows
✓	Focus of major political, economic and social decisions	✗	Remote from decision making leading to a sense of alienation and lack of power
✓	Good infrastructure and amenities	✗	Poor infrastructure and amenities

The most obvious disadvantage of peripheral areas, from a manufacturing and service delivery standpoint, is their remoteness from mass
markets. This is often coupled with a remoteness from suppliers of raw
materials and components. Together these factors mean higher transporta-
tion costs, placing firms located within the periphery at a comparative
disadvantage in today's highly competitive environment.

Peripheral areas often lack effective control over major decisions
affecting their economic and social well-being. The major decisions tend to
be taken at the core, where the key economic and political institutions are
based and the headquarters of major companies are located. As a consequence, organisations and individuals within the periphery often feel a
sense of alienation, a feeling of governance from afar and a lack of control
over their own destiny.

Internal economic linkages tend to be weaker at the periphery than at the core. The weakness of regional multiplier effects is a salient characteristic. Thus, for example, whereas the creation of an economic activity in the core will probably encourage other activities there, the creation of economic activities in the periphery will tend to have comparatively limited secondary impacts within the hinterland. Material flows will tend to be between the core and the periphery, rather than within the periphery.

Migration flows tend to be from the periphery to the core. This is probably the most dramatic characteristic and it is readily demonstrated by the sustained population drift from rural areas to urban centres in developed countries and by the mass migrations that have occurred from peripheral countries to their core counterparts. Irrespective of the destination, the outcome is a loss of people from the younger, more active and more talented segments. Since many peripheral areas are also important tourism destinations, they are often seen as good retirement locations. Although on the face of it this can help to counteract the effects of outward migration, the inflow of older people serves only to exacerbate the imbalance caused by the loss of young people.

Peripheries are characterised by a comparative lack of innovation. New products, new technologies and new ideas tend to be imported rather than developed within the periphery. To a large extent, this results from the fact that productive and managerial resources are concentrated at the core.

Information flows within the periphery and from the periphery to the core will be weaker than those from the core to the periphery. People within industrial south Wales may be more informed about events in London than they are about what is happening in more rural northern parts of their own country. Conversely, residents of London will often have comparatively little up-to-date information on what is happening in Wales, prompting them to place a greater reliance on impressions which are long established and possibly stereotypical. Thus, for example, the many people who regularly make the comfortable two-hour train journey from Cardiff to London, take in an all-day meeting and then return home early that evening are familiar with expressions of surprise from fellow delegates who find it hard to believe that such a schedule is commonplace and that Wales is not as far away as they had imagined.

Government may be required to play a greater role in promoting economic development in the periphery than in the core. Industrial south Wales, for example, was one of the first four areas to be designated to receive government assistance under the Special Areas Act 1934 and, more recently, specialist agencies have been established in both Scotland and Wales to help regenerate the economy. In Italy the *'Cassa per il Mezzogiorno'* has been established to promote the disadvantaged South.

Peripheral areas are also distinguished by their geographical characteristics. They are often noted for the beauty of their landscapes and seascapes, which may be expressed in a very dramatic way. Their physical character –

perceptual and actual – is often described using such stereotypical terms as *wilderness, remote, off the beaten track, the back of beyond* and *unspoilt*.

Issues for tourism

Wanhill (1997) identifies the following as being the main tourism issues facing peripheral areas in Europe, suggesting that local differences are usually a matter of degree:

- the alternative is usually an extractive (primary resource) economy with a small manufacturing base;
- there are limited market opportunities or markets have declined;
- delivery of the product is usually through small and medium enterprises (SMEs), with their attendant difficulties;
- there is a lack of tourism infrastructure or obsolete product;
- there are weather restrictions on the length of the season, as in Northern Europe;
- remoteness and strong natural environments are a product plus;
- environmental threats to undisturbed wilderness are likely;
- the social impact on small, close-knit communities can be great;
- the community lacks education, training, capital (public and private) and entrepreneurship, which mitigates against business formation; and
- there are limited organisational structures, lack of planning, direction and little statistical information.

We now turn specifically to Wales, a country on the periphery of Europe, starting with an examination of its tourism industry.

Tourism in Wales: An Overview

Wales, a small country of some 2.8 million people, along with England, Northern Ireland and Scotland, forms part of the United Kingdom. It bears many of the hallmarks of a peripheral area, insofar as it is located on the western edge of Europe next to a larger neighbour. In European terms, it forms part of the Atlantic Arc region which takes in the western part of the UK, as well as Ireland, the west of France, the north west of Spain and the whole of Portugal (Commission of European Communities (CEC), 1994). The regional grouping exhibits many of the typical characteristics of peripherality, including:

- a pattern of urban development clustered around cities of relatively modest size;
- relatively poor (but improving) transport links with European capitals and within the areas concerned;
- a higher dependence on traditional (and declining) manufacturing industries;

- a greater reliance on tourism, which tends to be concentrated on coastal locations and heavily dependent upon the traditional family market.

Tourism is a well-established industry in Wales and its structure and organisation is well documented. The Wales Tourist Board's medium-term policy document, *Tourism 2000 – A Strategy for Wales*, provides a good insight into contemporary policy issues and the following introduction to tourism in Wales draws heavily from it (Wales Tourist Board (WTB), 1994).

Volume and value

In relative terms, tourism is far more important to the economy of Wales than it is to other parts of the UK. Provisional figures estimate that spending from day and staying visitors to Wales in 1996 totalled £1.9 billion, an increase of 13% over 1995 and representing about 7% of GDP. Tourism supports some 90,000 jobs in Wales, about 9% of the workforce (WTB, 1997). The domestic market remains by far the largest source of business for Welsh tourism. According to the joint United Kingdom Tourism Survey, 11 million overnight tourist trips to Wales (for all purposes) by UK residents generated spending of £1718 million in 1996, which represents 8.5% of total domestic tourism spending within the UK (WTB, 1997). Wales has traditionally performed far less well in overseas markets. The last full year for which official statistics are available is 1995 when, according to the *International Passenger Survey* conducted by the Office for National Statistics, Wales attracted 740,000 overseas tourists, whose total expenditure amounted to £203 million. The latest figures from the joint *United Kingdom Day Visits Survey* show that day visitors to and within Wales spent some £550 million in 1996 (WTB, 1997).

Accommodation

A joint research initiative by the WTB and local authorities in 1989/90 identified a total accommodation capacity of 523,291 bedspaces in Wales (WTB, 1991). Self-catering forms of accommodation predominate in Wales: the WTB's product database, which concentrates on commercial accommodation enterprises, reveals that no fewer than 46% of all bedspaces were in caravans and camping and a further 21% in other forms of self-catering accommodation; the remaining 33% were in serviced accommodation enterprises (WTB, 1994).

A significant proportion of Wales' serviced accommodation bedstock remains concentrated in traditional resorts, built during Victorian times. Establishments tend to be small and privately owned. Traditionally targeted at the domestic family holiday market, resorts have found it more and more difficult to compete with competition from overseas destinations. Considerable investment has taken place to refurbish and improve the accommodation base, aided by financial assistance from the WTB, other official sources and the European Union. This has helped resorts to extend the season and to win new markets (e.g. conventions), although some remain economically fragile. Concurrently, there has been an upsurge in new hotel development within key urban areas such as Cardiff and along major strategic corridors. This has enabled Wales to attract more business travellers and short-break visitors, lessening its dependence on the family holiday market.

The self-catering sector is very diverse in terms of its product. The scale of operations varies and so does product quality. A large proportion of self-catering accommodation is located at or near the coast, with large scale caravan parks a prominent (and often intrusive) feature of some areas. Like the traditional resort hotel product, much of Wales' self-catering stock was originally developed to serve the needs of family holiday visitors, drawn from conurbations in Wales itself or adjacent regions of England. Many caravan parks and self-catering complexes have been upgraded substantially, but there remain a number of poorer quality operations, which the WTB acknowledges to be ill-equipped to meet the needs of modern markets (WTB, 1994). The self-catering sector has been especially reliant on long-stay visitors in the past, and operators have found it more difficult than their serviced counterparts to develop short-break products aimed at winning new markets.

The natural and built environment

Wales is a beautiful country, well endowed with natural resources for tourism and recreation. There are three National Parks covering an area of 4098 km^2. There are also other wide areas of countryside which have attractive, sometimes fragile landscapes and many of these carry some other form of designation. For example, there are five designated Areas of Outstanding Natural Beauty and if their land area of 949 km^2 is added to the National Parks, it will be seen that a quarter of the land area of Wales has been singled out for quality special environmental protection – a higher proportion than in other parts of the UK. There are 14 designated areas of Heritage Coast, covering 492 km of coast.

The built environment also forms an important part of the tourism infrastructure. There are 380 Conservation Areas and over 14,000 buildings have been listed as being of architectural or historic importance by Cadw (Welsh Historic Monuments, the official body responsible for such matters in Wales). Wales is especially well known for its castles, which are an evocative and sometimes contentious reminder of a turbulent past. Among them are the four World Heritage Sites at Caernarfon, Conwy, Beaumaris and Harlech. There are a number of attractive market towns in Wales, while resort towns such as Llandudno, Tenby and Llandrindod Wells are good and vibrant examples of the changing face of tourist resorts.

Attractions

According to the WTB's records, there are some 420 managed tourist attractions in Wales, about 50% of which submit information on their annual attendance. Museums and art galleries are in the majority (37%), followed by historic attractions (27%). Some 15% of attractions have a countryside theme and the remaining categories include restored railways (8%), craft facilities (5%), wildlife attractions (4%), leisure/fun facilities (3%) and industrial attractions (2%). About two-thirds of Welsh attractions receive fewer than 50,000 visitors per annum, highlighting the fact that this is a disparate and, in the main, small-scale sector. Nevertheless the six attractions with more than 300,000 visitors account for more than one in five of all the visits made to Welsh attractions, indicating their disproportionate importance.

Culture and language

Although constitutionally linked with England and an integral part of the United Kingdom, Wales has its own identity and a distinctive cultural tradition. Wales is very proud of its antecedents as a Celtic nation and it retains a close affinity with other similar areas such as Cornwall, Scotland, Ireland and Brittany.

Wales is a bilingual nation. English is spoken universally and, according to the 1991 Census, 508,098 – or 18.4% of the people of Wales aged three and over – spoke Welsh. The proportion of people speaking Welsh varies considerably from one area to another. In the so-called Welsh heartland areas (which are concentrated in the more rural north and the west of Wales) the language is spoken by 70% or more of the population. Considerable efforts are being made to revive the language after a period of sustained decline. According to the Welsh Language Board (WLB, 1995), the official body responsible for promoting the language, the situation of the language has been stabilised and the decline which has been evident since the beginning of the century has been arrested. The Welsh language is seen by the WTB as an important expression of the country's cultural identity, and it is thought to provide important opportunities for promoting Wales as a distinctive tourism destination, especially within key overseas markets (WTB, 1994).

Organisation of tourism

Within the UK there are four co-equal tourist boards set up under the Development of Tourism Act, 1969 – the British Tourist Authority and the English, Scottish and Wales Tourist Boards. They are pre-dated by the Irish Tourist Board, which was set up in 1948. As an independent statutory body, the WTB receives most of its funding from the Welsh Office, and its Chairman and board members are appointed by the Secretary of State for Wales. Under the 1969 Act, the British Tourist Authority was given sole responsibility for promoting Britain abroad, while the national tourist boards for England, Scotland and Wales were charged with promoting their own country within Britain and also undertaking a range of development and research related activities.

Each of the national tourist boards reports to a different Cabinet department. Over time, each board has evolved in a different way, reflecting the specific priorities of its sponsor department and its own view of future strategic priorities. The WTB is unique among the national tourist boards in that it continues to pursue all the key activities which it inherited at its inception. Neither the English nor the Scottish boards continues to offer financial incentives to assist new capital developments in tourism as provided for under the 1969 Act. Moreover, under the Tourism (Overseas Promotion) (Wales) Act 1992 the Wales Tourist Board acquired the power to undertake its own marketing activities overseas, to supplement the work of the British Tourist Authority. This strengthening of the role of the WTB came at a time when the powers and budgetary resources of the English Tourist Board, in particular, were being eroded. It suggests a greater recognition among successive Secretaries of State for Wales of the importance of tourism as a key industry and it also implies a recognition on the part of government that tourism in Wales is more vulnerable and deserving of a greater measure of support. On this evidence, it would appear that the WTB is seen by government as an effective and cost-efficient agency.

The Five Case Studies

As indicated earlier, the substantive part of our chapter takes the form of five separate case studies, drawing upon recent research at the University of Wales Institute, Cardiff. They are the product of separate investigations, which remain in progress, and they share a common interest in some aspect of tourism in Wales.

The five case studies presented here are each authored by the principal researcher associated with the project. These individual contributions are acknowledged by providing author attribution for each case study in addition to the comprehensive author citation for the chapter as a whole.

We have already reviewed the arguments for a clear distinction between core and peripheral regions. The fundamental truism of inequality and the spelling out of the realities of the relationship between core and periphery in economic and social terms lie at the heart of previous analyses of the concept. In this final section we seek to test the validity of those arguments against what we see happening in respect of tourism in Wales. In doing so we are operating in what Blomgren and Sørensen (1998: 10) call *'spheres of convergence'* between the conceptual/factual and the speculative/reflexive perspective on peripherality. In order to move our analysis beyond the boundaries of Wales we frame these case studies within two themes:

Theme 1: A paradox: tourism and development at the periphery

- Case Study 1: Visitor and resident place perceptions of Mid Wales (Louise Emanuel)
- Case Study 2: An examination of Wales' peripheral status in terms of information flows (Nicola Foster)

Theme 2: Transformation in the urban core – implications for the periphery

- Case Study 3: People, place and consumption (Martin Selby)
- Case Study 4: Cultural change and the re-positioning of Rhyl as a seaside resort (Tim Gale)
- Case Study 5: Public perception and measurement of coastal pollution at identified beaches in South Wales (Cliff Nelson)

Theme 1: A Paradox – Tourism and Development at the Periphery

The basic core–periphery model assumes for simplicity that each is a homogeneous entity, whose character and appearance set it apart from the other. In practice, of course, the situation is far more complex. Within any so-called core location there are pockets exhibiting tendencies towards peripherality, at least in relative terms. The converse is true of those regions whose general location and overall demeanour mark them as being peripheral.

The situation is further complicated by the fact that when an area engages in economic development it will wish to press home its comparative advantage (real or perceived) over competing regions. On the face of it, core regions will generally come out best in such exercises, being able to point to a strong economic record, a large market base, good transport links, an adaptive labour force and so on. However, when it comes to tourism development, these core attributes may or may not be assets: thus, while the promotion of a brand image based upon easy access and a vibrant city life makes eminent sense to an area wishing to develop business or short-break urban tourism, the archetypal periphery attributes of peace, quiet, fine scenery and traditional rural values are major strengths when it comes to targeting the growing market for activity holidays, away from it all.

When a nominally peripheral area such as Wales seeks simultaneously to attract tourists and to broaden its manufacturing base by encouraging new manufacturing and service industries, it will wish to tailor the message to the recipient, by emphasising core attributes to some and peripheral attributes to others. Quite clearly, the trappings of peripherality which a tourist may find appealing in a rural area may prove anathema to the prospective industrial investor – and, for that matter, to the resident. Some of these tensions are clearly illustrated in the studies by Emanuel and Foster, both of which in their own ways point to a paradox of tourism at the periphery.

Case Study 1: Visitor and resident place perceptions of Mid Wales (Louise Emanuel)

Scope of the research

The research investigates visitor and resident place perceptions of Mid Wales, and evaluates the potential of such perceptions to shape economic development in the area. A review of the literature indicated a need for an holistic approach to place. It was suggested that a starting point towards achieving this is to envisage place as three components – the real, the expected and the perceived. The real place was described using secondary statistical information and maps of the area. The expected place was described using topographical writing and guide books. The perceived place was examined through a combination of questionnaires and interviews with residents and visitors. These investigate perceptions of the landscape and economy of Mid Wales. The perceived places of residents and visitors are described. A number of agencies based in Mid Wales were also interviewed to examine (1) their perceptions of Mid Wales, (2) the way in which visitor and resident perceptions are incorporated into the policy development process and (3) their responses to some of the preliminary outcomes of the research.

Some relevant findings

The research concluded that both residents and visitors have well defined, but different place perceptions of Mid Wales. Visitor perceptions are more affected by the expected place than the real, while resident perceptions are more affected by the real than the expected. There are currently few mechanisms by which place perceptions are directly incorporated into the development process. However, the place perceptions of agencies were found to be close to those of the groups they represented; it is suggested that place perceptions are fundamental truths shared by groups, which are so strong as to actually subconsciously drive the policy development process.

Mid Wales, the study area of the research, bears many of the characteristics of the periphery. Predominantly a rural area with a low population density, it has an ageing population structure resulting both from out-migration of younger people and the appeal of the area as a retirement destination. For most of the last century Mid Wales has been experiencing depopulation; it enjoys poor communications and infrastructure, which can lead to isolation and poor access to social and cultural facilities. The problems of communication and isolation may also contribute to the lack of opportunities in the area, although in June 1991 Powys' unemployment rate was only 4.4% in relation to a figure of 8.5% for Wales as a whole (Welsh Office, 1991). These figures mask the real trend of outmigration which Mid Wales has been experiencing.

The dearth of opportunities in the area has created a vicious circle – unemployment is being exported, but this means depopulation and an ageing population structure which in itself diminishes the area's potential for attracting inward investment. However, as with many other peripheral areas, ironically it is this same isolation and rurality which have helped make the area attractive to tourists. As a consequence, tourism has grown in importance and remains one of the key forms of economic development encouraged by the local authorities in the area.

Periphery, by definition is a matter of location, but it is also a matter of perception. For those who are born and live there it is often envisaged as being disadvantaged in terms of access to social, cultural and economic activities; conversely, for those who visit the periphery, it is the same remoteness which prompted the journey. The study illustrated that these two groups, residents and visitors, have quite different perceptions of periphery, derived from their particular role within the environment. For example, there is an interesting difference in the way in which visitors and residents approached the idea of tourism in relation to landscape. While visitors seem to view tourism as a response to the landscape, in empathy with it, residents view it as an economic option. Visitors regard landscape as something to be gazed at, venerated and protected for future visitors, while residents are more likely to view it as a resource which can be manipulated to encourage tourism as a source of revenue. For some residents, the landscape was, in fact, perceived to be a debilitating factor with regard to employment creation because of the lack of infrastructure and poor communications which, in turn, have led to outmigration. Additionally, although landscape was felt to be a consideration in the siting of industry, it was by necessity a secondary one. The need to improve opportunities in the area, and subsequently reduce the inequalities between core and periphery was the residents' primary consideration for the future of the area. This need for positive development of the area was expressed by all residents interviewed, and was strongly emphasised by one in particular:

> 'Unless much more effective effort is made to employ local youngsters in worthwhile jobs with a career, I can only see stagnation – economic stagnation and a gradual deterioration in the infrastructure, businesses won't come here because although we have good roads, they are rather long – unless you have lived here you don't appreciate the disadvantages. We lose the best of the youngsters, when they've been to college they don't come back ... we have an ageing population with fewer and fewer attractions for outside business. I can't see it going any other way unless there are effective steps to keep youngsters here.'

However, while residents felt a strong need to encourage economic development in the area, visitors appeared to want to protect the landscape and disallow any form of development, seemingly not considering the needs of the local community. For visitors, Mid Wales is an almost idyllic retreat made special by its lack of industry and people, and by its remoteness. It is almost a living museum in which they lose themselves for a few days each year, and many of the visitors interviewed expressed an almost egotistical view that the landscape is solely there for their enjoyment. One visitor did perceive these attitudinal differences and said:

'I am very anti trying to keep things static – everyone has the right to economic well-being. Careful management is about looking after land, it's not a question of either/or. People who don't live in industrial landscapes often don't regard the needs of people living there. Visitors or holiday home owners often want an area to be kept as it is, putting it in a museum without a thought to the local economy.'

Visitors and residents often have different experiences of and requirements from an environment, and will subsequently perceive it in different ways. Understanding this, it is evident that tourism in the periphery becomes a paradox. While residents look towards tourism as a method of alleviating some of the inequalities caused by poor communications and access to opportunities, for visitors this remoteness is the tourism product itself. In effect, the factors which characterise the periphery are also positive contributors to its emergence as a tourist destination.

Case Study 2: An examination of Wales' peripheral status in terms of destination information flows (Nicola Foster)

Scope of the research

It is acknowledged that peripheral status holds implications for destination information flows. Using the example of Wales this research examines the way in which location on the periphery can result in a lack of awareness within potential markets and a low level of international tourism exposure. The main focus of this exploratory study surrounds Wales' performance vis-à-vis England and Scotland. A systems approach is applied and the perspectives of different tourism stakeholder groups are considered, namely: destination government agencies; destination-based tourism enterprises; tourist intermediaries; and tourists themselves. The findings are considered in relation to Wales' peripheral destination status.

Some relevant findings

Wales' position as a traditionally economically disadvantaged region of Britain is mirrored in its international tourism status. Table 1.2 illustrates that Wales' share of overseas visitors to Britain was significantly lower than that of England and Scotland (Office for National Statisitics, 1996). This situation is not new: year upon year Wales has attracted significantly fewer overseas visitors than England and Scotland. The difference cannot be explained simply in terms of the geographical location and relative size of the three countries and it is necessary, therefore, to explore other reasons.

Table 1.2 Volume and value of overseas visitors to England, Scotland and Wales

Country	Trips (000s)	Nights (m)	Spend (£m)
England	20840	198.3	10698
Scotland	1960	20.2	865
Wales	740	5.5	203

Historically Wales' low level of international tourism success may be recognised as a partial consequence of possessing little direct control over its overseas marketing. Under the 1969 Development of Tourism Act, responsibility for promoting Britain overseas was vested solely in the British Tourist Authority (BTA) and it was not until the Tourism (Overseas Promotion) (Wales) Act 1992, discussed earlier, that the WTB was enabled to undertake its own overseas marketing activity to supplement the work of the BTA. Thus, the control of information flows regarding Wales as an international tourist destination has traditionally been centralised in London. Although the BTA will justifiably wish to emphasise that it has not sought to neglect Wales in any way, the act of granting supplementary overseas marketing powers to the WTB implies a tacit acceptance by government that further steps were needed to enhance awareness of Wales overseas.

The WTB has argued that the key factor explaining the comparative lack of success in international tourism markets is a lack of awareness of Wales as a distinct entity rather than negative perceptions of the country. By nature, awareness must precede image. According to the World Tourism Organisation (WTO, 1970) an image can exist only if there is at least a small amount of knowledge. Milman and Pizam (1995) argue that for a tourist destination to be successful, it must first have a level of awareness, and second a positive image. A link between awareness, image, and destination popularity has been recognised in terms of the selection of holiday destinations both by consumers and tourist intermediaries (Goodall, 1990; Kent, 1990). Theoretical underpinnings of the concept of destination choice sets imply that a level of destination awareness must exist before that destination can be considered in a trade-off selection process. At the most basic level a destination must be known to exist. The absolute level of awareness that is necessary for a place to be recognised and selected as a potential tourist destination is problematic. This case study examines views on the relationship between Wales' peripheral destination status and the existing awareness levels of the destination via consultation with potential US tourists, US tour operators and Welsh tourist enterprises.

A brief questionnaire was devised in order to gauge the level of awareness of Wales amongst potential American visitors. The survey was administered via electronic mail using Internet news-groups as a sampling frame and 38 responses were received over a two-week period. Twenty-seven respondents reported that they had visited the UK. Of these, 12 reported having visited Wales and thus having first-hand experience of the country. Thirty-four respondents provided images of Wales, and the image–awareness link proved complex. All of the respondents who had visited Wales were able to provide an image of the destination; however, a large proportion of non-visitors to Wales also reported an image. The most remarkable finding was that 89% of the respondents who had not visited Britain were able to report an image of Wales, while only 13% of respondents who were familiar with Britain but not Wales reported an image of Wales.

These findings question the extent to which the images of one place may inadvertently be affected by experience of another. Previous experience of Britain did not appear to affect respondents' ability to provide an image. The images supplied by non-visitors to Wales often contained expressions of doubt but, even so, their content did not vary greatly from the images supplied by those who had previously visited Wales. All images were overwhelmingly positive. So why does Wales remain a less-visited British destination?

Weak destination information flows were recognised. Some of the respondents who found it difficult to provide an image of Wales remarked how the destination does not have strong exposure in America:

> 'information on Wales is difficult to come by in the States, and Wales doesn't make the evening news very often … not much of an international identity, I guess … no mark of distinction, like Scotch wiskey [*sic*] or British cars …'

Commercial supply of Welsh products by international tourism intermediaries is weak compared with England and Scotland. An analysis of 14 1997 US tour operator brochures offering packages to Britain as part of their programmes revealed that Wales featured as a separate destination in the programmes of three tour operators, whereas Scotland and England featured as separate destinations in the programmes of six and 12 tour operators respectively. Therefore, Wales' role in an American inclusive tourist circuit of Britain may be recognised as peripheral.

Comments were collated from 62 US tour operators to establish awareness of Wales and information flows were identified as a notable weakness:

> 'Lack of information in the US. Americans are generally ignorant about the differences between English, Welsh and Scottish heritage, culture, geography. English identity overwhelms the whole of the UK …'

> 'Factors limiting more extensive travel to Wales include the little Americans know of Wales compared to what they know of England and even Scotland.'

'Wales will continue to be the poor relation in terms of tourism from the USA until the tourist board markets to the public in a more aggressive manner (best example is the Irish Tourist Board).'

'Tour operators are not in a position to increase demand to a destination of which there is negligible public awareness.'

The ownership structure of Welsh tourist attractions is highly fragmented and operators are heavily reliant upon the WTB as a vehicle for promoting their enterprises to overseas markets. Of the 518 listed Welsh tourist attractions 296 provided a written input to the research. Of particular relevance to the theme of this study is the widely held perception that both external and internal information flows are not strong enough:

'Welsh tourism is very poorly presented and has virtually no professional marketing compared to Cornwall or Ireland. In comparison our place in the marketplace is non-existent.'

'I do believe that the Wales Tourist Board needs to review its marketing strategy and also its communication (or lack of) with attraction operators and resorts …'

However, despite being critical of WTB marketing efforts operators acknowledged the need to increase awareness of Wales in a responsible manner:

'Please don't promote Wales too much and turn it into a scenic park!'

This research indicates that tourism stakeholder groups perceive a lack of information about Wales as a tourism destination, particularly in comparison with its neighbours within Britain. Although the relative unawareness of Wales is a contributory factor to Wales' peripheral destination status, it is clear that the undeveloped nature of the destination is perceived by some as a strong positive asset. In the short term the threat of over-promotion is not a serious one: the immediate priority is to enhance awareness of Wales as a distinctive destination within Britain. Redressing the situation will take time: the resources of the BTA and WTB are finite and it is not easy for Wales to make its voice heard within a large and noisy market place. While recognising that this is a major challenge, the WTB (1997) remains optimistic, recording in its annual report that:

[O]n the basis of statistics available for the first nine months of 1996, the Board is predicting a 19% increase in overseas visitor numbers and spend which is forecast to reach £240 million. This will represent the fourth successive year of growth from overseas markets, the most important being the USA, Germany, France and Australia. The indications are strong that Wales will have performed significantly better in 1996 than the UK as a whole where spending from overseas visitors is only forecast to increase by 6%.

Theme 2: Transformation at the Core – Implications for the Periphery

The description in our introduction of the core–periphery distinction suggests a concrete and unchanging scenario. The utility of such an approach to clarify the construct may at one level hide a more complex picture. In contrast to the simple conceptualisation given earlier, this analytical theme takes as its starting point a notion of dynamic between the core and the periphery. As Selby points out in the third case study, policy decisions have been taken at the core which are intended to reduce the disadvantage felt at the periphery. Yet serious decline in the economic condition of the urban core has created conditions within the core that might be considered indicative of greater deprivation than that of peripheral areas. Under an analysis that subsumes a change, the distinction between core and periphery becomes considerably blurred. Moreover, the difficulty in influencing the real conditions of the periphery through centrally derived policy intervention has, along with several strands of political thought about the nation-state and regionalism, resulted in a transition in the political arrangements surrounding core–periphery relations. The creation of a new political Assembly for Wales in its capital, Cardiff, is just one indicator of the devolving of greater responsibility for governance to the regional level in the UK. As a result the debate in Wales has shifted from its peripheral status within the UK to a debate about core–periphery relations within Europe. This is most strongly demonstrated in Wales' relations with the structural funds of the EU, where the relative buoyancy of the economy of South East Wales threatens to take Wales out of any future map of regional support within Europe. That map is set to expand to include the new nations of the former Soviet bloc and, thereby, to become coloured by a different magnitude of disadvantage.

It follows that changes in the economic conditions within the core, combined with spatial realignments of what is core and periphery, create the dynamic around Wales' status in any core–periphery axiom. This dynamic is, we argue, a reflexive one in that what happens within one element affects the other. To take the examples given thus far, change in the economic conditions of the urban core of British cities alters our perceptions of disadvantage in rural Wales, while the expansion of the EU to include eastern Europe questions the conceptualisation of what is core and what is periphery in western Europe. At first sight, changes in economic conditions, political relations and spatial scale threaten the very validity of the construct. We argue, however, through the following case studies, that conceptualising the core–periphery construct as if in transformation rescues and strengthens its value to understanding tourism.

The studies by Gale and Nelson speak of transformation in rather different senses. Gale's study of a seaside resort in the periphery seeks to understand the transformation of the fortunes of the resort. The periphery is in many senses a playground for the populations of the core and the growth, prosperity and decline of Rhyl, Gale argues in Case Study 4, is predicated upon the social and cultural conditions at the core. What then happens to Rhyl if and when those conditions change? Gale's argument is that it is not that Rhyl is part of a general condition of peripherality that is important to understanding its past, present and future as a tourist resort but that its transformations are directly related to a set of social, economic and cultural transformations at the core. Nelson's study also displays the same sense in which the periphery as the supply side of tourism is in a dynamic relationship with the demand side as represented by the mass of population living at the core. His case study is of a transformation in cultural values and of resultant political actions. First, the rise of environmental consciousness among urban dwellers has resulted in a new politics of the environment. This, combined with the rise in consumer consciousness, has resulted in a perceived importance of health risks for consumers of the environment. In an ironic twist what was once seen as a cure for ill health – a dip in the sea – has now become positively unhealthy. The political initiative has been taken up by government on a supranational scale by the EEC through the bathing water quality legislation. The prevalence of coastline within the periphery of Europe of course means that it is in the periphery that the legislation has its most impact and Nelson's study offers an evaluation of the effectiveness of the legislative activities of the core from the perspective of the periphery. It is the sense in which each of these studies reminds us of the reflexivity in the dynamic of the relationship between core and periphery that enables us to speak of transformation.

Case Study 3: People, place and consumption (Martin Selby)

Scope of the research

This project examines place images and place consumption in Cardiff, the capital city of Wales, in the context of urban tourism. The city's status in terms of the core–periphery model is an important element of the research. The aim is to evaluate Cardiff in terms of both first-hand experience of the landscape or the *'place product'*, and images in the potential market influenced by representations of the city. The first phase established an inter-subjective language of tourism decision-making, consisting of salient factors used in distinguishing between urban destinations. Sixty repertory grid interviews were conducted in Cardiff and in two of the city's competitors – Bristol and Edinburgh. In the second phase of research, over 400 surveys were completed in the same locations to compare and contrast the images between different groups of place consumers.

Considerable attention has been paid to discrepancies between images inside and outside the city, and these shed light on Cardiff's status within the core–periphery model. The combination of methodological techniques was influenced by a critical review of prevailing epistemologies in a number of disciplines, none of which was considered capable of conceptualising the city as consumed. Although the data analysis revealed some subtle influences on the experiences of different groups of place consumers, some interesting general insights into Cardiff's core–periphery status also emerged. These relate to both Cardiff's *'place product'* and to naive images associated with representations in the potential market. Although Wales as a whole might be considered peripheral in terms of its remoteness and relative rurality, Cardiff falls into the group of post-industrial localities targeted by the European Union's Regional Development Fund. The priority for cities such as Cardiff has been restructuring and industrial diversification, including tertiary sectors such as tourism. Furthermore, images held by tourists are considered to have implications for the sustainability of inward investment in general. As authors such as Collinge (1989) have argued, in the era of footloose capital, an attractive place to visitors is often also attractive to investors.

Some relevant findings

It has been estimated that Cardiff's tourism generates £144 million of direct expenditure each year, supporting over 5000 jobs (L & R Leisure, 1995). In 1994 the WTB set a target for Wales to attract 11.1 million visitors by the year 2000, with Cardiff acting as an important gateway with *'a critical mass of tourism, cultural, and leisure facilities'* (WTB, 1994). Recent figures show that some of these targets are already being reached, with annual visitor increases of over 30% at several of the city's attractions.

Data from the urban tourism study at UWIC appear to reinforce much of this optimism, and question Cardiff's peripheral status. The data, analysed with a combination of the use of image indices and factor analysis, indicate that perceptions are overwhelmingly positive, with expectations consistently exceeded. Hardly symptomatic of widespread de-industrialisation, there are very high levels of satisfaction among visitors to Cardiff. The historical gems, particularly the castle, are extremely well regarded by both domestic and overseas visitors, along with the *'impressive'* civic centre and museum. Rather than being marred by the scars of heavy industry, Cardiff is rated highly in terms of its parks and surrounding countryside. Visitors generally experience a *'safe'* and *'friendly'* city, and consider it to be *'unique'*. Although some longer-term visitors expect a greater variety of arts and cultural facilities, Cardiff's four main festivals undoubtedly provide additional variety. Among the small percentage of visitors with negative perceptions of Cardiff, it would not appear that it is the city's peripheral status which is the problem. More a cost of economic activity than inactivity, visitors are clearly concerned about the traffic congestion in the heart of the city. The majority of both domestic and overseas visitors, therefore, appear surprised to find a thriving and impressive Welsh capital, with an interesting and unique identity.

The data from the tourism study and the buoyant state of the capital's economy in general would not seem to be characteristic of a peripheral city. Although Cardiff suffered during the 1970s, like many British cities, its economy has been immensely healthy over the longer term, in both relative and absolute terms. Between 1951 and 1981, for example, total employment grew by 17.7%, and population grew by 12.3% (Hausner, 1986: 30–1). During the same period employment in London and the major British conurbations fell by over 15%. In this context it is not surprising that Wales consistently gains more than a fifth of all inward investment to the UK (Middleton, 1991: 123). With the success of industrial diversification, one could assume that urban tourism has had an effective synergistic role in a buoyant economy, forming an important element in the wider place marketing and economic development effort. Despite this apparent success in the tertiary and quaternary sectors, however, there are also indications that would seem to support Cardiff's peripheral status. The city attracts less than half the volume of visitors than does Edinburgh, and lags behind Bristol. The tourism and leisure sectors are growing, and they are significant, but so they are in numerous cities, in the UK and abroad.

There continues to be a great deal of debate about the image of Wales and its perceived lack of a clear brand identity. This debate certainly seems pertinent to Cardiff, as the data on naive images from outside Cardiff are permeated by a severe lack of awareness. In contrast to Scotland, with the world-renowned Edinburgh as its gateway, very little is known about Wales or Cardiff among potential visitors from overseas. Even among those who have heard of the capital, many would expect to find relatively little of interest. Despite Cardiff's location, only two hours by rail from London, its relative accessibility is rarely recognised, possibly because of the city's exclusion from the established overseas tourist circuit.

The domestic market's naive images pose even more of a problem. Somewhat ironic in the context of the core–periphery debate, is the finding that Cardiff is more likely to be perceived as *'industrial'* than be associated with its parks or surrounding countryside. It would seem that more persistent images are of heavy industry and coal. The city is not considered to be particularly accessible, and even when it is, accessibility can actually have negative connotations, being associated with over-familiarity. Familiarity in the form of the Max Boyce syndrome[1] does appear to breed contempt amongst domestic visitors without first-hand experience of Cardiff. These organic images from a range of sources appear to be deeply sedimented in the *'stocks of knowledge'*[2] of many potential visitors. While such images may be too strong to transform with limited promotional budgets, the representations associated with them certainly deserve further research. Domestic images, therefore, including those of the Scottish and Irish, pose particular problems. While a lack of awareness can be built upon, undesirable images may first have to be demolished.

There are a number of possible explanations for the inconclusive evidence regarding Cardiff's core–periphery status. Taking the optimistic interpretation, there is no doubt that Cardiff has been more successful than many post-industrial British cities in restructuring its economy. The city once relied on a handful of staple industries – in the 1920s half the male population worked in steel, mining, shipping and the railway (Middleton, 1991: 120). Diversification has been extremely successful, and tertiary sectors such as tourism have prospered.

It would appear that at least part of the explanation relates to strong and coherent regeneration initiatives. Ambitious plans are being put in place to re-develop the city's maritime quarter, after a long period of neglect and decline, under the leadership of the Cardiff Bay Development Corporation.

Evidence in support of Cardiff's peripheral status would seem to centre around the argument that, despite a relatively resourceful programme of regeneration, the city is still perceived as peripheral from outside. This would appear to be the case both in Britain and overseas. A more cynical explanation of high levels of inward investment might include both low wage levels and immense financial inducements by government. In the pessimistic scenario, Cardiff is performing relatively well economically, yet only as the capital of a small, rural and peripheral country on the wrong side of the UK. The inconclusive evidence, however, may point towards a third explanation, and one with fundamental implications for the core–periphery model itself. Since its conception in the 1940s, the model has been applied to a bewildering range of scales. In the 1970s, however, the core–periphery concept became somewhat stretched, with the emergence not only of underdeveloped rural districts in spatially marginal areas, but also de-industrialised areas which were previously part of, or very close to, the core. Although the constantly shifting axis came as no surprise, and the model was still driven by the notion of economic disparity, the conceptualisation became somewhat less succinct. In the postmodern/post-industrial era, where the spatial mobility of capital is ever increasing, images and representations of localities from outside have become fundamental to economic development. The emergence of one more dimension within the core–periphery model further blurs the spatial metaphor, and it is rather difficult to accommodate. This could eventually be enough to seriously question the continued validity of the core–periphery concept.

Case Study 4: Cultural change and the repositioning of Rhyl as a seaside resort (Tim Gale)

Scope of the research

Elsewhere in this chapter, the inequalities that distinguish peripheral from core areas have been explained with reference to economic, demographic and political arguments. In this contribution, we shall see how cultural developments have diminished the appeal of seaside resorts within Wales and Britain, which can be said to be peripheral both in terms of location and character. Reference will be made to the findings emerging from an ongoing research project. Its aim is to interpret the influence of late 20th century cultural (and social) change upon the identity and image of an established resort (Rhyl), focusing upon the involvement of the local authority in the material and symbolic transformation of the tourism resource. Located on the north Wales coast, Rhyl has a resident population of 24,909 and (together with its smaller neighbour Prestatyn) attracts 1.7 million staying visitors and 2.5 million day excursionists per annum.

The methodological approach chosen for this venture is a semiotic analysis of the resort's landscape as text, and the representations of that landscape in place promotional literature (the annual municipal brochure, to be precise), for the period 1935 to date. Semiotics, or the science of signs, is a method of interpreting the meanings implicit in acts of communication and representation, which would normally be taken at face value. These acts, or signs, are notionally divided into two components for analysis: the *signifier*, or expression, and the *signified*, or represented concept. For any given sign, the relationship between signifier and signified tells us much about the culture to which that sign belongs, particularly where that relationship is arbitrary or conventional (e.g. the brochures of the British tour operator Club 18–30 not only signify male and female tourists on holiday, but ideologically motivated conceptions of freedom from the behavioural constraints of everyday life, and the promise of sexual adventure).

The choice of methodology and analytical focus has been made with a view to achieving the following objectives:

- to identify and interpret signs of Rhyl's status as a tourist destination, and the prevailing tenets which fashion the experiences and practices of its visitors – furthermore, to extend this analysis historically, accounting for variations in the material and symbolic existence of Rhyl as evidence of sociocultural change;
- to ascertain the direction and extent of local authority involvement in the provision and promotion of the elements which comprise the Rhyl product; and
- to compare the identity, or physical reality, of Rhyl with the image depicted in the written, visual and verbal discourse of those charged with promoting the resort to would-be tourists, explaining any differences that may exist between referent and sign.

Some relevant findings

Between 1979 and 1988, the number of visitor nights spent at British seaside resorts declined by 39 million, or 27%. In Wales, a lesser reduction (13%) was noted for the same period (WTB, 1992). Drawing an analogy between the urban areas of tourist residence as core, and the seaside resorts as periphery, it is possible to see why this took place. During the 19th and early 20th centuries, the two areas enjoyed a mutually beneficial relationship: capital flowed into the periphery in the form of tourist spending and investment by wealthy industrialists, and productivity gains were noted at the core among employees who had recently returned from a holiday by the sea.

The Industrial Revolution created the circumstances whereby the seaside became favoured as a destination for the masses. Key factors were improved incomes for the working classes, a flourishing railway network with high passenger capacity and low fares, the demand for holidays as a means of (temporary) escape from the poor living and working conditions of the manufacturing towns and cities, and greater entrepreneurial involvement and leadership on the supply side of the tourism industry, with improvements to the provision of seaside accommodation, attractions and organised excursions. Above all, the distinctive natural qualities of the coastal environment, combined with the unique forms of pleasure consumption offered by the piers, theatres, funfairs, botanical gardens, holiday camps and the like, set seaside resorts apart from other urban areas of Britain, this very contrast constituting the attraction of places such as Rhyl before the mid-1970s.

The recent paradigm shift in social and cultural arrangements, popularly branded as post-modernism, has contrived to weaken this distinction. The relevant constructs of post-modernism may be summarised as follows (Urry, 1994):

- There has been a substitution of a culture of writing and substance with one of image and surface meaning, where the consumption of cultural products is reduced to spectacle and play. In this context, the derivation of aesthetic pleasure is no longer limited to the seaside, given that new technologies can mechanically replicate the objects of visual and tourist consumption in any place, urban or rural, which is repositioning itself as a visitor destination (e.g. Wigan Pier, Alton Towers or the Center Parcs Holiday Village in Sherwood Forest).
- The compression of geographically and historically distant events into the *here and now*, aided by faster and more extensive transport and communications systems has provided a new set of travel and entertainment opportunities which compete effectively with existing resorts.
- Consumption and recreation are increasingly relevant to the formation of social identity, as opposed to the once-dominant influences of occupation and the home, leading to increasingly flexible, complex and unstable personalities, with less established and routine patterns of travel behaviour.

- Production and consumption within western economies has become post-Fordist in nature, as a shift in employment from manufacturing to service and information industries, has seen the dissipation of associated work and leisure practices, the partial rejection of products developed for mass publics and the nostalgic veneration of traditional working life.
- Finally, a fresh emphasis upon the local, as a response to the crisis of place identity brought on by globalisation, might work in favour of those seaside resorts which have lost much of their sense of place through insensitive modernist planning and construction. However, it is equally likely to benefit other peripheral places, such as heritage towns and the countryside, at a time when distinctiveness is an essential element in capturing commercial investment and tourist interest.

The effect has been the displacement of what Turner and Ash (1975) term *'the pleasure periphery'* over greater distances from the main areas of residence, as initially the most affluent tourists, and later the proletariat, showed a greater tendency to substitute for the British seaside an expanding range of more exotic and unspoilt (overseas) locations, made accessible by time–space convergence (Goodall, 1992).

Those seaside resorts where much of the traditional long-holiday family trade has been lost to competitor destinations, illustrate the contradictory nature of Friedmann's downward transition region (see Haggett, 1983). On the one hand, they possess all the defining criteria of periphery: high unemployment, dependency upon a declining industry, an elderly population, visual signs of urban decay and neglect and the likelihood of assistance from the public sector. Yet, on the other, the most important, and benign, inequality between seaside periphery and urban core has been compromised, namely the exceptional leisure landscapes of the former. This is a result of the inevitable economic and social problems that arise when a high-capacity built environment is under-used by those for whom it was designed and of the appropriation of many of the seaside's distinguishing features for pleasure consumption at the core. Thus, all cities now possess amusement arcades, bingo halls, live entertainment, a variety of gastronomic opportunities and well-developed accommodation and retailing functions.

From the research it is possible to identify four key elements of the tourism resource which indicate these processes of divergence and convergence:

- *Attractions and amenities*. Rhyl, like many resorts, has seen the removal of several seaside attractions of old, on the grounds of falling revenues, visual dilapidation and safety concerns: the pier was demolished in 1973, followed by the Pavilion Theatre in 1974 and the Royal Floral Hall in 1990. A new breed of post-modern attraction has taken their place: the Sun Centre opened in 1979 (a wet weather facility comprising a soft-edged swimming pool with simulated waves and tropical heat), the Rhyl museum in 1988 (a celebration of the resort's past, with a representation of the old pier and displays of seaside paraphernalia), the Skytower in 1989 (a 240 foot import from the Glasgow Garden Festival) and the Children's Village in 1995 (a collection of retail units, whose spectacular Disneyesque architecture masks an otherwise mundane collection of retail units and the tourist information centre, not to mention a large debt for the local authority). Although these function as markers for the new 'Rhyl', they might be construed as less extraordinary, given the similarity of their design and interpretation to attractions in non-resort locations, and their apparent incongruity with the existing geographic properties of the seaside.

- *Land use.* An audit conducted in 1997 of the properties along Rhyl's West Parade, once almost exclusively occupied by providers of tourist accommodation (by virtue of commanding a sea view), revealed an interesting mix of tourism and non-tourism functions (ground floor usage only). Of the 70 separate properties surveyed, there were 14 amusement arcades, 13 retailers of consumer goods and souvenirs, 13 vacant or derelict structures, 12 food and drink providers (not all licensed), 10 private residences and a mere eight guest houses and hotels (some providing board for the homeless, as opposed to tourists). This is an expression of several trends at the seaside: the rapid fall in serviced accommodation (as self-catering and caravan parks have grown in popularity), a bias in visiting custom towards the lower end of the market, the increase in permanent residency (notably on the part of the economically disadvantaged) and a lack of private-sector involvement in the tourism product.
- *Infrastructure.* The motor car revolution, and the parallel decline of rail travel, has left its mark on Rhyl, by introducing to the coastal environment the seasonal, and typically core problems of exhaust pollution, congestion and severe competition for parking space. Fortunately, the resort retains its rail service, by virtue of its location along the strategically important North Wales main line. It is better placed than resorts left isolated by the pruning of the branch line network, which has reinforced their peripheral status and removed one of the earlier catalysts of their development.
- *Built environment.* The quality and distinctiveness of much of Rhyl's townscape has been impaired by insufficient investment and attention in earlier years, followed later by unfavourable adaptations to the original Victorian and Edwardian architecture. The ambience of the town has not been improved by the construction of characterless apartments and blocks of flats, and the unsympathetic redevelop-

ment of the core shopping zone. Rhyl is certainly not alone in this respect: many other towns have experienced very similar problems. Vigorous attempts have been made by successive local authorities to rejuvenate the resort, aided by substantial financial assistance from such sources as the Welsh Development Agency, the WTB and the European Community. They have partly addressed these problems, with an architectural emphasis upon the vernacular (the restoration of indigenous built form, using local building materials and reintroducing ornamental detailing) and the spectacular (as in the case of the Children's Village and Events Arena).

Case Study 5: Public perception and measurement of coastal pollution at identified beaches in South Wales (Cliff Nelson)

Scope of the research

A multidisciplinary project was initiated to examine health effects of bathing in sewage contaminated coastal waters, using a popular beach resort close to the cities of South Wales called Barry Island, and to explore ways of measuring public perception of coastal pollution at selected beaches in South Wales. The research also investigates the regulatory framework responsible for the sustainability of coastal tourism and the effectiveness of beach award flags as marketing tools in the promotion of resorts.

Current legislation addresses coastal pollution in terms of physical health criteria with little regard given to aesthetic quality of sea/landscape and psychological well-being of the beach consumer. In this study it is argued that it is necessary to cross the boundaries between the social and physical sciences in order to take an holistic view of the coastal scene, accounting for environmental, political, economic and social aspects. To achieve the aims of the study the following objectives were formulated:

- to determine recreational water quality at the resort of Barry Island;
- to investigate whether an exposure/disease relationship exists between swimmers and non-swimmers;
- to gauge perceptions of coastal pollution along the South Wales shoreline; and
- to gain a knowledge of the level of understanding and attitudes to seaside award schemes across different beaches.

Some relevant findings

The issue of bathing water quality is of universal concern to maritime tourism destinations. National governments and the European Union have become increasingly involved in trying to find solutions to the problem of worsening water quality (CEC, 1976, 1991). The increased political interest in bathing water quality is indicative of a broader environmental concern by governments. It is also a response to vigorous and informed campaigning by individuals and organisations. The effects of such legislation may be felt disproportionately in the periphery, where natural environments are the norm. Political influence over the periphery can, therefore, be seen as synonymous with economic core–periphery relations.

What seems to be absent from the attempt to find solutions to the bathing water quality issue is any attempt to assess how legislation designed to improve the situation and emanating from the core is actually affecting the periphery. This study attempts to begin this process in the case of Wales by drawing upon data being gathered as part of the previously described project. Two impacts of the legislation upon the situation in Wales are explored, one intended and one unintended. The intended drive to measure the quality of bathing water has resulted in a number of beach award schemes and the general understanding of these schemes by tourist consumers surveyed in the study is discussed. The second impact we would argue is the unintended consequences of the interaction between the economic interests of both the tourism and environmental industries.

Sun, sea and sand have provided an attractive cocktail to tourists since Victorian times, providing an irresistible source of pleasure for day and holiday visitors drawn largely from core industrial conurbations. At that time a day at the beach was believed to be so beneficial to health that '*trips to immerse oneself in salt water were completed with almost missionary zeal*' (Rees, 1993). More recently, adverse publicity about the condition of British beaches (*Independent on Sunday*, 1994) and, in particular, poor water quality has not been conducive to public confidence (Kay *et al.*, 1994). These have all added to the problems of traditional resorts in Britain which were already finding it difficult to compete with overseas holiday destinations, offering attractive holiday packages at a very competitive price (see Case Study 4).

As indicated earlier, Wales is a country of great natural beauty with a diverse coastline. The beaches found along Wales' 1284 km of coast vary greatly in terms of their character. At one end of the spectrum there are resort beaches with a wide variety of visitor facilities such as car parking, toilets, shops, restaurants and lifeguards. At the other extreme are the small, often remote beaches whose main appeal is their lack of amenities and sophistication. The great majority of Wales' beaches fall into the latter category, and this has an important bearing on their performance in beach award schemes whose criteria embrace on-shore facility provision as well as water quality.

Concern has been expressed regarding the proliferation of official and voluntary schemes in Britain seeking to monitor water quality and classify bathing beaches. Although their aims are laudable – namely to give objective advice and information on issues considered by their proponents to be central to public safety, peace of mind and enjoyment – their very profusion and complexity may produce entirely the opposite effect. This prompted

Owen (1994) to issue the following challenge to an audience drawn from the various official, private and voluntary sector organisations concerned with coastal management in the UK:

> How many of us here today, I wonder, would relish the challenge of describing clearly and simply on one sheet of A4 paper – without conferring and without notes – the precise purpose, modus operandi and inter-relationship between the EC Bathing Waters Directive, the European Blue Flag Scheme, the Seaside Award Scheme, the Norwich Union Coastwatch UK Project, the Heinz Guide to British Beaches and the Reader's Digest Good Beach Guide? If today's audience baulks at that task, what do you imagine will be the response of the general public, as the intended beneficiaries of these schemes?

A small part of the study has been to examine the effectiveness of beach award schemes in terms of understanding and knowledge for influencing consumer behaviour. The results of this work suggest that public aware-ness of the different beach award schemes is low. Of the different types of award schemes included on the questionnaire, the European Blue Flag Award scheme gained highest recognition, but even those that identified with it often had a misunderstanding of its true meaning. A worrying finding was that a number of the visitors interviewed on the beach believed the blue flag to represent danger rather than any measure of bathing water quality. On this evidence, more needs to be done by the relevant official, private sector and environmental bodies to inform consumers of the purpose and scope of the various schemes. If consumers misinterpret the meaning of the flag which flies on a designated beach, then the designation of the beach will do little to offset consumers' concerns about health risks.

Bathing water and beach quality initiatives typically have their origins at the core rather than at the periphery. This is especially true of European initiatives such as the Blue Flag Award, which forms part of the supra-national framework of environmental protection, and it also applies to UK-wide initiatives, such as the Seaside Award scheme developed by the Tidy Britain Group. Although it can justifiably be claimed that the achievements of key voluntary groups such as the Tidy Britain Group and the Marine Conservation Society are a good example of public-led environ-mental innovation, some would argue that such initiatives often derive from intellectual stimulus more typical of the urban core than the rural periphery.

In Wales, however, we are beginning to see something rather different occurring, whose roots lie firmly within the periphery itself. The Green Sea project is a partnership of official, private and voluntary sector bodies, chaired by the WTB. As well as Dŵr Cymru-Welsh Water (the private utility company responsible for providing water and sewerage services to the public and to industry) the initiative includes local authorities, environmental agencies, business organisations and a large number of voluntary and campaigning groups. Launched in 1996 and named after a Dylan Thomas poem, it has been described in these ambitious terms (Dŵr Cymru-Welsh Water, 1997):

> The aim of Green Sea is to make the coastline of Wales the pride of Europe. [It] is a unique joint venture involving more than 30 public and private organisations which are concerned with the environment ... Green Sea will protect a national asset of incalculable value, ensuring the highest environmental standards around the coast.

Green Sea has evolved from Dŵr Cymru-Welsh Water's commitment to improving coastal sewerage treatment (1995–2000) to a level where water quality at Welsh bathing beaches complies with EC Guideline Standards, some 20 times more stringent than the legally required EC Mandatory Standards under the European Bathing Water Directive (FEEE, 1996; Green Sea, 1997). Guideline standard bathing water quality is the minimum needed for Blue Flag status, and the key goal is to win 50 of these for Wales by the year 2000. Although the number of Blue Flag beaches has risen slowly over the years, the number stood at a modest nine in 1997 and so the target remains an ambitious one.

The positive alliance found in the Green Sea initiative between environmental agencies, campaigning groups and tourism promotion agencies within Wales is novel and to be commended. It challenges those who seek to dismiss tourism simply as a commercially dominated agent of environmental degradation. Its partners recognise that there are mutual benefits to be gained in working towards a politically desirable and consumer-orientated end. The tourism organisations recognise the importance of sustaining environmental quality in the fight for tourist consumers – and as an asset to be prized for its intrinsic worth. Their partners from the official and voluntary environmental groups, for their part, appreciate that tourism is an important and legitimate industry, whose well-being depends upon the existence of a clean and safe environment.

The cost of achieving 50 Blue Flag beaches for Wales will be substantial. Dŵr Cymru-Welsh Water's total investment in coastal projects over the next five years will be more than £600 million, equivalent to £500 for every household in Wales. Against this background, it is very reassuring to know that research conducted in September 1995 showed that 61% of people in Wales are not satisfied with the quality of sea water in our bathing areas and 96% think it is important that this is improved (Dŵr Cymru-Welsh Water, 1996).

It can be argued that the core stands to gain more than the periphery from these developments. Perhaps cynically, some might claim that the main beneficiaries will be persons from other parts of Britain and further afield who account for the majority of Wales' tourists. Another interpretation might be that the economic benefits will accrue mainly to the construction industry and the suppliers of sophisticated water treatment technologies, possibly as an economic leakage from the coastal periphery itself to the urban core beyond Wales. It is not proposed to develop these arguments further, for fear of being thought to be placing the economic well-being of the host community above the physical health of the public at large. The Green Sea Initiative is to be welcomed, recognising as it does that the environment deserves to be maintained for its own sake and that it is an important tourism resource. However, the full potential benefits of cleaner bathing water will accrue only if those who aspire to use Welsh beaches fully understand the aims and significance of the various beach commendation schemes. This research suggests that consumer awareness is presently very low. Allaying fears of health risk is important in ensuring tourists will want to visit beaches in the future. Just as a belief in the health benefits of immersion in sea water led to the creation of coastal resorts then the fear must be that the counterargument will hasten their demise.

Conclusion

In conclusion, we in Wales have welcomed the invitation to imagine ourselves at the periphery and to think about our collective work in tourism using this construct. The exercise has proved to be a creative adventure of the imagination. The evidence from Wales suggests that the simple distinction between core and periphery hides a much more complex picture.

Notes

1. Max Boyce is a Welsh singer and entertainer whose act contains numerous references to rugby, coal-mining and the traditional culture of the Welsh industrial valleys.
2. The concept *'stock of knowledge'* is taken from Schutz (1970, 1974) and refers to the knowledge of a phenomenon acquired inter-subjectively by individuals. Also known as *'social knowledge'*, it is commonly acquired through the organic representations produced by the media, education, government and other institutions.

References

Begg, I., Moore, M. and Rhodes, J. (1986) Economic and social change in urban Britain and the inner cities. In V.A. Hausner (ed.) *Critical Issues in Urban Economic Development, Vol. 1*. Oxford: Clarendon Press.

Blomgren, K.B. and Sørensen, A. (1998) Peripherality – factor or feature? Reflections on peripherality in tourism research. *Progress in Tourism and Hospitality Research* 4, 1–18.

Brunet, R. (1989) *Les Villes Européenes*. Paris: La documentation Française, RECLUS, DATAR.

Burton, I. (1971) The social role of attitude and perception studies. In W.R.D. Sewell and I. Burton (eds) *Perception and Attitudes in Resource Management* (pp. 37–54). Ottawa: Information Canada.

Collinge, M. (1989) *Tourism and Urban Regeneration. Vision for Cities Conference*. London: English Tourist Board.

Commission of the European Communities (1976) Council Directive of 8 December 1975 concerning the quality of bathing water (76/160/EEC). *Official Journal of the European Communities*, 5 February. L31/1 5/2/76.

Commission of the European Communities (1994) *Competitiveness and Cohesion: Fifth Period Report on the Social and Economic Situation and Development of the Regions in the Community*. Luxembourg: Commission of the European Communities.

Commission of the European Communities (1991) Council directive concerning urban waste water treatment. *Official Journal of the European Communities* (91/271/EEC). L/135 30/5/91.

Dŵr Cymru-Welsh Water (1996) *Customer and Environment Report 1995–96*. Brecon: Dŵr Cymru-Welsh Water.

Dŵr Cymru-Welsh Water (1997) *The Green Sea Initiative*. Brecon: Dŵr Cymru-Welsh Water.

DCC (1995) Prospectus. Unpublished.

Foundation for Environmental Education in Europe (1996) *The Blue Flag Campaign*. FEEE, European Office, Denmark.

Fisher, A. and Raucher, R. (1984) *Intrinsic Benefits of Improved Water Quality: Conceptual and Empirical Perspectives, Vol. 3*. Wesport, CT: JAI Press.

Goodall, B. (1990) Opportunity sets as analytical marketing instruments: A destination area view. In G. Ashworth and B. Goodall (eds) *Marketing Tourism Places* (pp. 63–84). London: Routledge.

Goodall, B. (1992) Coastal resorts: Development and redevelopment. *Built Environment* 18, 5–11.

Green Sea News (1997) Cardiff: Wales Tourist Board.

Haggett, P. (1983) *Geography: A Modern Synthesis*. New York: Harper Collins.

Independent on Sunday (1994) Survey shows British beaches make you sick (30 January).

Kay, D., Fleisher, J.M., Salmon, R.L., Jones, F., Wyer, M.D., Godfree, A.F., Zelenauch-Jacquotte, Z. and Shore, R. (1994) Bathing water quality. *The Lancet* 344, 905–9.

Kent, P. (1990) People, places, priorities: Opportunity sets and consumers' holiday choice. In G. Ashworth and B. Goodall (eds) *Marketing Tourism Places* (pp. 42–62). London: Routledge.

Kilby, M.C. (1980) *Industrial Investment: Must Britain Always Lose Out?* London: Association of British Chambers of Commerce.

L & R Leisure (1995) *Cardiff Strategic Tourism Plan Report*. Cardiff

Middleton, M. (1991) *Cities in Transition: The Regeneration of Britain's Inner Cities*. London: Michael Joseph.

Milman, A. and Pizam, A. (1995) The role of awareness and familiarity with a destination: The central Florida case. *Journal of Travel Research* 34 (3), 21–27.

Office for National Statistics (1996) *The International Passenger Survey*. London: Office for National Statistics.

Owen, R. Elwyn (1994) Coastal management – a tourism perspective. Norwich Union Coastwatch UK Conference on Public Participation in Coastal Management, May.

Rees, G. (1993) Health implications of sewage in coastal waters – the British case. *Marine Pollution Bulletin* 26, 14–19.

Schutz, A. (1970) *Reflections on the Problem of Relevance*. New Haven: Yale University Press.

Schutz, A. and Luckmann, T. (1974) *Structures of the Life-World*. Transl. G. Walsh and
    F. Lehnert. London: Heinemann.
Turner, L. and Ash, J. (1975) *The Golden Hordes: International Tourism and the Pleasure
    Periphery*. London: Constable.
Urry, J. (1994) Cultural change and contemporary tourism. *Leisure Studies* 13, 233–8.
Welsh Language Board (1995) *A Strategy for the Welsh Language*. Cardiff: WLB.
Wales Tourist Board (1991) *Final Report of the All Wales Tourism Working Party's
    Visitor Stock Survey*. Cardiff: WTB.
Wales Tourist Board (1992) *Prospects for Coastal Resorts – A Paper for Discussion*.
    Cardiff: WTB.
Wales Tourist Board (1994) *Tourism 2000 – A Strategy for Wales*. Cardiff: WTB.
Wales Tourist Board (1997) *Annual Report 1996/97*. Cardiff: WTB.
Wanhill, S. (1997) Peripheral area tourism. *Progress in Tourism and Hospitality
    Research* 3, 47–70.
Welsh Office (1991) *Digest of Welsh Statistics*. Cardiff: Welsh Office.
World Tourism Organization (1980) *Tourist Images*. Madrid: WTO.

Chapter 2

PACE: Guiding Rural Tourism Development in a Fragile Area

MARCUS GRANT

This chapter presents a method for Project Appraisal and Community Evaluation (PACE) which is being piloted in the Avalon Marshes, which lie in the internationally important wetlands of the Somerset Levels and Moors. The Levels and Moors occupy some 900 km^2 in the County of Somerset (Southwest England) and contain low-lying areas of moor, much of which has been drained for agriculture and urban flood relief. The themes discussed here include:

- how to move from sustainable tourism theory to practice;
- the role of a lead authority as initiator and coordinator;
- mechanisms for facilitating wider access to decisions that will have strategic implications.

The two elements, the land and water, shift and exchange, muddle in with each other and then separate as the creeping growth ... tries to re-establish the solid in this would-be liquid. (Sutherland & Nicholson, 1986)

The evocative name '*Avalon Marshes*' was chosen because it conjures up a picture of this wide bottomed valley in the Somerset Levels as it was in ancient times – a vast expanse of marshland surrounding an island sea, alternately flooded by fresh and salt water. For over five millennia humans have wrestled with the forces of water here, in what was, for most of this time, an area difficult to penetrate. Archaeology has uncovered remains of early trackways linking settlements across the treacherous bogs and marshes. The Avalon Marshes, like many of the world's great wetlands, has remained an area of peripherality. The isolated culture that evolved was uniquely moulded to this wetland lifestyle. This culture has been documented in the local museums of the area, through photography and in prose. The Avalon Marshes are also of international importance in containing statutory protected areas, e.g. a National Nature Reserve and several Sites of Special Scientific Interest, with parts also falling into an EU Birds Directive Special Protection Area (SPA) and Ramsar site.

The Avalon Marshes are typical of many similar peripheral areas in that they face pressures for development resulting from the need for increases in employment, changes in agriculture, development of tourism and nature conservation; the resolution of these are crucial to their social, environmental and economic future. The nature conservation interests, in particular Bird Life International (known as the Royal Society for the Protection of Birds or RSPB in Britain), are interested in developing and piloting a project appraisal which could be applied to other peripheral areas with important and fragile natural environments.

In the Avalon Marshes, the economic base relied on increasingly in the latter half of the 20th century, in this case large-scale peat excavation and EU subsidy-supported farming, is in decline; local rural employment is increasingly scarce; higher values are being placed on the area's contribution to biodiversity. Moreover, through national guidance and the local planning system, the criteria for reclamation of the industrially derelict land and support of farming practices are now geared towards the delivery of biodiversity objectives. It is partly the high quality of the nature conservation resource in the area that has led to pressure for tourism development as local businesses seek new opportunities through nature tourism. However, its assets are not just limited to nature conservation. As a result of the preserving qualities of peat and connections with the myths of King Arthur and Avalon, the area generates international archaeological and historic interest. The Arthurian legends lead to a steady flow of independent youth travellers from Europe, North America and the Antipodes. Attractive too is the unique cultural landscape, based on the traditional way of life of relatively low-intensity farming and peat-cutting. Also potentially relevant to tourism development are the abundant water supplies and *'holes in the ground'* (worked out peat pits) making fishing and recreation lakes relatively cheap to implement.

Somerset County Council, the strategic planning authority, set out the parameters for reclamation of the peat works with a plan for basic zoning which envisaged a nature conservation core and a buffer where wetland-compatible recreation would be appropriate (Somerset County Council, 1992). Development of any kind needs to be undertaken very carefully in this fragile environment. To provide jobs in tourism, slowly reduce reliance on peat-cutting and increase nature conservation value require certain changes in the infrastructure and land management practices. However, both the wetland ecological assemblages and preserved archaeological resource are vulnerable to water level and water quality. The cultural landscape is vulnerable to incremental change and poorly thought-out development. The early 1990s saw a period of extensive research (an environmental science-based base-line report by Somerset Country Council established basic hydrological and ecological parameters (Halcrow-Fox, 1992); this was followed by a multidisciplinary planning, economic and land-use analysis (Land Use Consultancy, 1994)) resulting in a vision for the area which contained a number of sensitive land use and employment options for consideration by local landowners and the wider community The vision helped to define the concept for the Avalon Marshes. It originally envisaged former peat workings becoming a restored wetland, with lakes and reedbeds primarily for nature conservation, with access and visitor facilities and compatible recreation activities, coupled to appropriate commercial activities.

The area embodies an example of Getz and Jamal's (1994) complex tourism 'domain, where no single individual, agency or group can resolve strategic tourism issues by acting alone'. The steering group of the initial options study previously referred to consisted of the representatives of some 15 different organisations or sectional interests, including two local authorities and one strategic planning authority, the statutory bodies for water, agriculture, nature conservation and local interests such as two internal drainage boards, the peat cutters and local land-owners' associations and otter conservation. This is a situation where there is a need for a new approach to tourism planning.

Recognising the need for cooperative working early in the 1990s, Somerset County Council initiated and led a consultative and representative process in the whole of the Somerset Levels and Moors called the Levels and Moors Project. The representative body, the Levels and Moors Partnership, is a non-statutory body involving representatives of communities, business and farming, nature conservation, water authorities and the planning authorities. A sub-group, the Avalon Mashes Advisory Group, is specifically concerned with the Avalon Marshes, where extensive wetland restoration is already underway (Taylor, 1997). The current project, sponsored by English Nature (the government's nature conservation advisors) and the RSPB, has sought to provide the Avalon Marshes Advisory Group with a framework for setting strategic goals and reviewing projects and proposals against those goals. Issues considered in the development of this framework included the following questions.

- How could the process deliver environmental, social and economic sustainability?
- Could a single mechanism be versatile enough to be rigorous for large proposals but not over-cumbersome and too bureaucratic for small-scale projects?
- Can a single process include review of both long-term programmes and review of specific projects?
- How can all interested parties, from parish councils to local and regional councils, from businesses to conservation bodies have access?
- How can a process meet the specific demands of rural tourism development?

The resulting framework consists of a tiered approach with three levels of assessment. The assessments are based on environmental assessment (EA) (the methods and processes used for examining how the existing environmental characteristics of an area are likely to be altered by human activity) but use a wider definition than the one used in the European Directive on Environmental Assessment and the UK Regulations (EEC, 1985; Town and County Planning Regulations, 1988).

The three tiers are:

- the strategic level relating to policies, plans or programmes – Strategic Environmental Assessment (SEA);
- major projects involving complex processes in sensitive areas – Environmental Impact Analysis (EIA);
- small-scale projects and proposals not requiring formal assessment – Project Appraisal and Community Evaluation (PACE).

Strategic Level Assessment

Strategic EAs examine the likely effects of policies, plans and programmes on the environment and a new Council Directive covering SEAs was presented by the European Commission on 4 December 1996 (EU, 1996). There is no formal requirement for SEA in the UK but government departments are encouraged to undertake environmental appraisals of new policies, and local authorities are asked to appraise development plans, using techniques which are closely analogous to SEA. The current project envisages that all of the agencies involved in developing the Avalon Marshes Strategy work together in developing an SEA. The aim will be to ensure that the activities of each agency are designed, wherever possible, to support and reinforce protection and enhancement of the environment.

Assessment for Major Projects

Large and complex projects which are likely to have significant effects on the environment are subject to formal EA under national regulations (e.g. Town and County Planning Regulations, 1988) and the European Council Directive (EEC, 1985). This framework recommends that whether or not formal assessment is actually required, the principles of environmental assessment should be applied to all projects within the Avalon Marshes, and should be introduced at the earliest opportunity, which is often the point at which the basic concepts and ideas are being formulated.

Assessment for Small Projects (PACE)

Many small projects have the potential to affect the environment of sensitive areas like the Avalon Marshes through both their direct impacts

Table 2.1 The three mechanisms for achieving sustainability in the Avalon Marshes

Component	Role in Avalon Marshes
Strategic Environmental Assessment (SEA)	Assessment of policies, plans and programmes arising from the aims of the Avalon Marshes. These are assessed against sustainability goals and against each other
Environmental Impact Assessment (EIA)	Assessment of (large) projects as required under EIA legislation
Project Appraisal and Community Evaluation (PACE)	Assessment of (small) projects not needing EIA and proposals at an early stage by the promoter or others to check compliance with the Avalon Marshes aims and sustainability

and also the cumulative effects arising from interactions between them. This provides strong grounds for considering the impacts of such proposals even though they are not covered by statutory regulations. Use of EA techniques is also valuable in improving the quality of the development proposal and enhancing its design.

A simplified form of assessment procedure has been developed, specifically for use within the Avalon Marshes area. We have called this type of assessment '*Project Appraisal and Community Evaluation*', partly to distinguish the method from the formal EA required on large projects, and partly to reflect the concern it shows for the local, social and economic context. Table 2.1 outlines the components of the tiered approach; although the main focus of this paper is PACE it cannot be viewed in isolation from the entire framework.

The Approach in Theory

Sustainability

All projects concerned with sustainability in tourism must also address the honing of the concept of sustainable development. It is over 10 years since the seminal definition of sustainable development as that 'which meets the needs of the present without compromising the ability of future generations to meet their own needs' (World Commission on Environment and Development, 1987). At first a polarised debate between the environmental and industry lobbies obscured the fact that sustainability also has a social dimension. It is now generally recognised that sustainable development recognises the validity of three interests – the environment, the economy and sociocultural concerns (Macgillivray & Zadek, 1995). In undertaking this project, EIA methodology was adapted, as it was a suitable model which had already been developed to address all three issues (Department of the Environment, 1989). In the context of the Avalon Marshes, where the strategic objectives embody biodiversity goals, environmentally sensitive development is not enough and the planning model has to help deliver biodiversity and/or other goals on the sustainability agenda.

In addition to the current task in hand, it has been suggested that sustainable development has its own self-referring agenda, an educative role, in helping broaden awareness of our place in the environment and so leading to a change in ethics (Hughes, 1995). In other words, the values implicit in sustainable development need to be communicated within the sustainable development project itself (IUCN, 1995). This was felt to be an important consideration in this project.

A review of the literature indicates that, in pursuing a sustainable approach, tourism development should:

- focus on small-scale, environmentally sensitive development (Burr, 1995);
- be integrated into the wider concerns of sustainable development (Hunter, 1995);
- use a sustainable approach for dealing with problems of rural tourism (Lane, 1994);
- involve and empower the local community (Burr, 1995).

Small scale

Without the right approach small scale can mean piecemeal. From early on in this project, the potential for tourism development on a small scale was seen as a problem and not, in itself, a solution. Land ownership is very fragmented in the Avalon Marshes, some large blocks of land are under single ownership but the majority of the land is a patchwork of small fields under various ownerships. The least beneficial scenario is that of a plethora of small landowners each using their meagre resources to develop the cheapest reclamation option, say a fishing lake with a small hut and car park. This would lead not only to an unacceptable loss in landscape quality but to fierce market competition which would minimise local economic gains. A previous study had already developed an overall vision and strategy for the area which, following public consultation, was increasingly winning support (Land Use Consultants, 1994). It was decided that to appraise small projects the process had to have:

- a method for testing each tourism proposal against the strategy;
- a method for the early assessment and mitigation of potential cumulative effects.

These two requirements are seen as essential to the process for two reasons. First, they can be used to ensure that projects allowed to proceed actually contribute to achieving the socioeconomic, biodiversity and strategic goals of the vision. Second, they allow for the assessment of projects in the pipeline or even at preparatory feasibility stages. This, in itself, can help minimise negative impacts and help promoters prepare a more appropriate project.

In terms of local economic development, recent empirical studies show that the small scale and soft options are likely to provide the greatest economic benefits (Slee *et al.*, 1996a). This emphasises the importance of finding a suitable planning and management process for the small scale.

Integrated studies

Vertical integration

The need for sustainable tourism to be seen as a sub-set of sustainable development has recently been restated (Hunter, 1995). In implementation this means that a sustainable tourism planning and management process must sit within a wider framework for sustainable development. In the Avalon Marshes a vertically integrated process was seen as the only approach, vertical integration being the term used for linking small local projects into wider project area concerns which, in turn, are linked with a set of regional objectives. This was needed to encompass the depth of awareness and process management required. To this end, the core of the process, PACE, which deals with projects and proposals, is embedded within an SEA, dealing with policies, plans and programmes.

Horizontal integration

Sustainable development aims to link economic, environmental and social factors into a mutually supporting process. Without a horizontally integrated process, there is the potential for the disparate groups of residents, wildlife interests, businesses and local government all to pursue conflicting agendas. A horizontally integrated process should include all issues – this will help to include all interested parties. For this kind of process to be a success, collaborative relationships need to be developed between all parties; the quality of these working relationships evolves over time (Getz & Jamal, 1994). This was recognised by the County Council early on in the process and led to the formation of the Levels and Moors Partnership, a forum for collaborative working. Through this, in the case of the Avalon Marshes, most of the interested parties had already been involved in some form of joint working. Continuing and consolidating this collaborative working was seen as an important goal in achieving an integrated process when set against the usual formal legal planning process which encourages an adversarial conflict between planning proposers and objectors. Therefore it was determined that to promote success, the PACE process should contain:

- components which encourage collaborative working, e.g. tasks suitable for joint working; and
- processes and tools to encourage consensus by allowing all parties to be heard and to respond to concerns while also acknowledging their common ground.

Rural tourism

Tourism in the Avalon Marshes is an example of rural tourism with rurality at its heart. In this context, Lane (1994) suggests that any approach should:

- have management systems to deal with problems relating to tourism penetration, e.g. traffic flows, access control, carrying capacities;
- be able to reconcile the tensions between the forces attempting economic growth to reverse rural decline and the forces of conservation and recognise the importance of involving local business and communities in ownership, decision-making and benefits;
- be able to maintain rurality in landscape and built form.

Lane postulates that a sustainable approach would be capable of fulfilling these requirements. Certainly the tiered approach, outlined earlier, with the PACE process sitting within a wider SEA process can address these requirements through having the capacity to monitor and control issues such as cumulative effects and patterns of growth over the longer term and across the whole project area.

Community tourism

The small scale implicit in community tourism has been dealt with earlier. However, two other community tourism factors are of concern. First, there is the likely style of tourism emerging with many community-based tourism providers, which has been referred to as 'soft' tourism (Slee *et al.*, 1996b). The term 'soft' does not necessarily mean environmentally or socially benign. Therefore the PACE planning process has been designed to be rigorous even in its evaluation of small-scale or soft proposals.

Second, consideration must be given to the mechanism for community involvement in the planning and management of tourism within the locality. In a study looking at the implementation of sustainable planning and design for tourism, citizen participation was found to be one of the six dimensions of sustainability (Knowles-Lankford & Lankford, 1995). Recognised also by the Local Agenda 21 programme, involving local people and listening to local concerns is now seen to have a legitimate role to play in sustainable development. But there are few models of a single planning process which will incorporate local interests (both positive and negative contributions) within a development strategy linked to local authority planning structures and systems. The regional planning process, in the study area, is typical of that found in much of England in that the county authority, in this case Somerset County Council, is responsible for strategic planning of the region through the production of structure plans. Linked to this, the district authorities provide further detail in their local plans. The plans are all produced, with consultation, on a cycle of about 10 years. New projects in the area from whatever source are presented as planning proposals and measured, together with any objections, against the adopted plans.

By involving the local and county planning officers in the development of PACE, their approval was sought to see its validity as a vehicle for reviewing projects, its usefulness in discussing and formatting objections and its capability for helping achieve strategic goals.

Community participation in impact assessment

It was quickly seen that the key to obtaining the required levels of community involvement was to ensure that the process recognised and protected the host community's quality of life. The criteria used for this should as far as possible come from the community and be voiced in its own words. Developing social criteria is essential to such an integrated planning process since host quality of life is an integral part of sustainable development (Christensen, 1995). The PACE process requires further work in connection with achieving this objective.

Community-level group involvement in impact assessment has an established tradition. Through action at public enquiries and protests, communities have often sought to give voice to the local economic, social and environmental consequences of development schemes. In a review of community participation in impact assessment, Runyan (1977) presents a range of tools available and scores them for usefulness in a local group setting. His criteria for usefulness, in community situations, are for tools that:

- are simple to use;
- do not rely on a database; and
- provide new insights and information.

He scores and ranks a number of tools. Several of the tools that are at the top of his table, such as checklists, IMPASSE and the Delbecq technique, play an important part in PACE.

The Approach in Practice: Description of PACE

The PACE process has been designed to be used by both promoters of projects and those concerned by their likely effects. It has been developed so that it is easy to use and will assist all interested parties either in preparing their own projects or in responding to new projects and proposals. It is intended that the process be refined and developed, by the lead authority, as experience in its application is gained. An outline of the basic components is given in this paper.

The primary responsibility for assembly of project information, its appraisal and production of a summary of that appraisal rests with a project's sponsor. Thereafter the information is transferred to a lead authority and, together with the results of parish and other consultations, is

Figure 2.1 Process for project appraisal for the Avalon Marshes

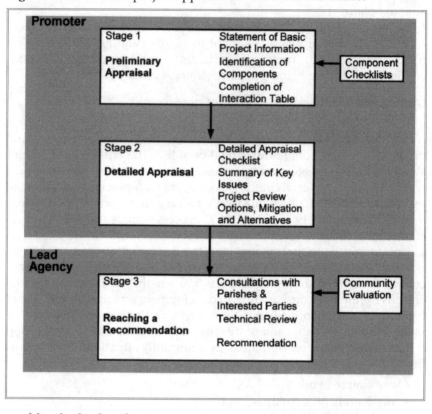

used by the lead authority to reach a conclusion and recommendations regarding the project.

The PACE process is worked through step by step for each project appraisal. For each step there are specially designed blank forms on which to collect and organise relevant information. There are also guidance notes. The steps to the complete assessment have been divided into four stages. Stages 1 and 2 (preliminary appraisal and detailed appraisal) are undertaken by the promoter of the proposed project. Stage 3 (evaluation) is carried out by the lead agency. Stage 4 (reaching a recommendation) is undertaken by the decision-maker. The process is illustrated in Figure 2.1.

At the heart of the appraisal is the testing of the project against environmental, social, economic and strategic issues. These issues have been divided into topic areas which embody both the indicators for sustainable development and the aspirations represented in the Avalon Marshes Strategy.

Stage 1: Preliminary appraisal

This stage, in three steps, clarifies basic project information, lists project components and identifies whether a detailed appraisal is required through review of the primary perceived impacts. The aim is to establish a clear description of the project though not to gather every available piece of information. Enough information is collected to clarify:

(1) the reasons for promoting the project and choice of location;
(2) the nature of the project (e.g. built form, scale, operations, lifespan); and
(3) the existing land conditions and environmental, economic and social concerns.

This initial stage of project definition indicates likely key issues, the depth of appraisal which is likely to be required and identifies any specialist resources that may be needed to carry out the appraisal. Having defined the basic nature of the project, a more detailed understanding of its key characteristics is built up. The main components of the development (e.g. built structures, infrastructure, business operations) are identified and listed, for both the construction and operational phases. All movements of people, machinery or materials on or off site are noted. The first stage finishes with the completion of an interaction table.

The interaction table will illuminate the relationships between components of the development and the environmental, socioeconomic or strategic topic areas. The vertical axis contains a list of the main project components. The potential impact topic areas have been set out along the horizontal axis. Topic areas have been grouped into sections covering environmental, social, economic and strategic issues.

Ease of use is aimed at by emphasising in the guidance notes that the process of compiling the table should be carried out rapidly but systematically. At this level of analysis it is only possible to draw preliminary conclusions about the level of significance, these can be refined in later stages of the appraisal. The results of the interaction table will show at a glance what the key issues are likely to be, and will help to determine the level of appraisal which is subsequently required. An example of a completed table can be found in Figure 2.2.

Stage 2: Detailed appraisal

The three steps in this stage provide a rigorous analysis of the perceived significant impacts at an early stage so allowing for amendment to project design and proposals for mitigation. It also provides information on which external parties will base their judgements.

Having completed the interaction table, a detailed appraisal of those areas which are considered to be the most significant should follow. This task is undertaken using the Detailed Appraisal Checklist. Each topic area

Figure 2.2 Example of an interaction table

INTERACTION TABLE

Topic Area **Indicate potential impacts by placing a 0,1,2 or 3 in the box** Development Characteristics	Environmental						Social			Economic		Strategic		
	Geology & Soils	Flora & Fauna	Water	Air & Climate	Landscape & Cultural heritage	Material Assets	Healthy Environment	Effects on Daily Life	Employment	Business environment	Existing & Potential Economic Land Uses	Inter-project	Cumulative Effects	Avalon Marshes Strategic Goals

Notes: Potential Significance of Impacts recorded as follows:

      3   Highly Significant
      2   Of Some Significance
      1   Of Little Significance
      0   Of No Significance

is represented at this stage in more detail as a series of indicators. This stage also calls for a more detailed examination of the levels of significance of impact between project component and the indicator to signify positive or negative effects and whether they are of major, moderate or minor significance. Whether the perceived effects of the project are likely to be adverse or beneficial, short or long term, of local or strategic significance, and reversible or irreversible are also recorded. The detailed checklist also provides space for a description of the nature of the effect, which should quantify values wherever possible and provide qualitative data if quantification is not possible. In some cases, completion of the checklist may identify gaps in information pointing up the need for further research. A single page from the 15-page detailed checklist is reproduced in Figure 2.3.

The information gathered in the detailed checklist needs to be analysed and presented in a way which helps to clarify the relative importance of individual impacts and establishes the key beneficial and adverse effects. This is carried out by ranking the relative importance of the effects that have been identified within the environmental, social, economic and strategic categories, producing a summary of key issues. The aim is to decide, for each category, which issues are likely to be of greatest significance to the Avalon Marshes. These are also likely to be the issues on which review of project design should be focused.

Once ranking has been carried out for each category, the key issues for project review need to be distilled. This is the final stage for the promoter before handing the document over to the lead agency. Project review by the promoter provides scope for making adjustments to project design in order to minimise the significant impacts.

Even following successful completion of this type of internal review, there will often be a number of residual impacts still associated with the project. This stage allows the promoter to put forward, for the consideration of the lead agency and other parties, options and proposals for mitigation and monitoring. Following this, the documents generated so far and the whole process is handed over to the lead agency.

Stage 3: Evaluation

This stage allows for the lead authority to circulate information and coordinate the responses. The completed forms from Stages 1 and 2 are used as a basis of gathering comments from the parishes and other interested parties. A questionnaire-styled form entitled *'Community Evaluation'* has been produced to assist the parishes in making responses within the timescale and constraints of a normal parish meeting. The form covers the same ground as the detailed appraisal but prompts for answers associated with locally perceived impacts. Other interested parties such as nature conservation bodies, local business interests or local authorities can use sections of the *'detailed proposal'* stages of the process to make their own

Figure 2.3 An example of a detailed appraisal checklist

DETAILED APPRAISAL CHECKLIST				
ENVIRONMENTAL TOPIC AREAS -	SIGNIFICANCE OF IMPACT (✓ if positive, ✗ if negative)			
5.0 LANDSCAPE & CULTURAL HERITAGE	Major ✓ or ✗	Moderate ✓ or ✗	Minor ✓ or ✗	NATURE OF IMPACT* (L/S St/Lt R/Ir)
5.1 **PPZs** Description of Impact :				
5.2 **ESA** Description of Impact :				
5.3 **AVALON MARSHES CONSULTATION AREA** Description of Impact :				
5.4 **LOCAL SETTLEMENTS & LISTED BUILDINGS** Description of Impact :				
5.5 **SCHEDULED ANCIENT MONUMENTS** Description of Impact :				
5.6 **SITES OF ARCHAEOLOGICAL IMPORTANCE** Description of Impact :				
5.7 **OTHER AREAS OF CULTURAL IMPORTANCE** Description of Impact :				
*KEY : L=Local; S=Strategic; St= Short-term; Lt=Long-term; R=Reversible; Ir=Irreversible				

comments. A typical page from the Community Evaluation form is reproduced in Figure 2.4.

Stage 4: Reaching a recommendation

The two steps in this final stage allow for the decision-maker to review the responses, from both the community and technical sources, and reach a recommendation.

On completion of this step, all the available information on which a recommendation by the lead agency will eventually be based should have

Figure 2.4 Community evaluation form

5.0 LANDSCAPE & CULTURAL HERITAGE		
Do you think that the proposed project will significantly change the landscape of the PPZs, ESA Areas or wider Avalon Marshes Consultation Area? If yes, please give details:	Yes	No
Do you think that the proposed project will bring any significant change to the character of the local villages and parish hinterland ? If yes, please give details:	Yes	No
Will the proposed project have any other locally important buildings, archaeological remains or other things of importance to the locality? (E.g. special trees, cross roads, verges) If yes, please give details:	Yes	No
6.0 MATERIAL ASSETS		
Do you think that the proposed project will adversely affect any other locally important assets? If yes, please give details:	Yes	No
SOCIAL & ECONOMIC IMPACTS		
1.0 HEALTHY ENVIRONMENT		
Do you think that the proposed project will increase the noise levels in the locality? If yes, please give details:	Yes	No
Do you think that the proposed project will lead to increased traffic in the parish? If yes, please give details and describe any specific concerns (e.g. dangerous junctions, parking):	Yes	No

been assembled. However, this information needs to be collated, analysed and presented in a way which helps to clarify the relative importance of individual impacts and establishes the key beneficial and adverse effects. This step has been called the technical review. The relative importance of the perceived effects is again ranked within the environmental, social and economic categories. This review combines material from the promoter's summary of key issues together with comments from the Community Evaluation form and forms received from other interested parties. The aim is to decide, for each topic, which issues are likely to be of greatest significance in reaching a decision on whether or not to take the development forward. Once ranking has been carried out for each individual subject, the key issues for making a recommendation are distilled. There is provision for three outcomes:

(1) approval of the project in the form proposed;
(2) rejection of the proposal outright;
(3) conditional approval of the project subject to mitigation, modification, relocation etc.

The reasons for reaching the recommendation can also be recorded on the form; a sample form is included in Figure 2.5.

Critique and Review of the Framework

Peripheral areas are often rural in character and can be areas with problems of social exclusion. There are often few opportunities for development, whether sustainable or not. In these areas, opportunities that do exist often revolve around the natural environment and because of the beauty and special character of a peripheral area, they may often involve tourism. These are communities which have few other options. In this context, a method such as PACE, which facilitates development in keeping with the natural, social and local economic assets (i.e. sustainable development) is vital.

Assessment of this approach is at an early stage and the PACE is still being piloted and refined. The RSPB and English Nature are reviewing its application for appraisal of their nature conservation initiatives in the area and local planning authorities are looking at its adoption as supplementary planning guidance. It has been used in the proposals for wetland enhancement in the Exminster Marshes, Devon and the regional RSPB office has an advocacy programme the objectives of which are to spread awareness and use of this method. At the time of writing, Autumn 1998, there is too little experience in its application for even a preliminary evaluation of its use.

Success will be partly dependent on take-up of the framework by the non-governmental organisations, business groups and parishes. Individually, they will benefit by having a systematic method for the assessment of their own projects and those proposed by other parties. If endorsed by the planning authorities PACE also gives local organisations a powerful method for commenting on the impact of other organisations' projects in a recognised format. As stated earlier, community involvement and small-scale sensitive development by local businesses are often thought to be the key to sustainable rural tourism; however, these ingredients are not enough. Communities and businesses require a tool assisting with the

Figure 2.5 Recommendation form

RECOMMENDATION

KEY ISSUES FOR DECISION-MAKING :

....

MITIGATION MEASURES OR MODIFICATION PROPOSED/REQUIRED :

....

MONITORING PROPOSED/REQUIRED :

....

RECOMMENDATION

☐ That project be approved as designed

☐ That project be approved subject to specific conditions on mitigation/modification(to be listed separately) *see above*

☐ That project be rejected

NO RECOMMENDATION REACHED

☐ A recommenadtion was unable to be reached at this stage (reasons listed below)

....

language, process and the political keys to dovetail into the local and regional planning systems. PACE has been designed to provide such a tool.

The framework has also been designed to take sustainable tourism theory out into the live development arena which contains many idiosyncrasies. Although the framework is robust, in being able to accept variety in the nature and scale of projects assessed, without wide sponsorship and understanding it could be at the mercy of vested interests, hidden political agendas or planning system inertia. What is required is investment from a lead authority, through either Somerset County Council, the Levels and Moors Partnership or the Environment Agency, in its continued maintenance, development and promotion. There are a wealth of benefits for the Avalon Marshes Advisory Group members in pursuing their shared vision of the Avalon Mashes. These include secondary benefits coming from easier communication among all participants through the use of a common approach for project review and assisting local communities and businesses in developing their concepts and visions of sustainability.

It is hoped that the process will also stimulate higher standards of development projects, as assessed against the Avalon Mashes Strategy objectives, through the possibility for early systematic appraisal and design alteration. This is seen as key by the nature conservation partners, since it guards against the more usual *ad hoc* and *post hoc* approaches to appraisal, where each project is likely to be assessed as a one-off, late-in-the-day effort, and the opportunity to use a continual stream of small proposals to achieve long-term biodiversity goals is lost. There will also be benefits from improved quality decision-making, through better provision of information and the adoption of a documented method for project appraisal which can then be improved and refined through experience.

Hopefully the link with the local authority planning structures will also be sufficient to provide enough carrot and stick to avoid '*the tragedy of the commons*'. Communally there is much to gain from the use of this process, but will the benefits to each individual organisation be sufficient to ensure take-up and so achieve the communal objectives?

Acknowledgements

Peter Nelson, a director of Land Use Consultants, led the project that developed PACE as a component within a Strategic Environmental Assessment (SEA). The author wishes to acknowledge his vital role in the development of PACE, the core structure of which was based on Land Use Consultants' previous work. Land Use Consultants has extensive and continuing involvement both in the subject of environmental assessment and with processes in the Somerset levels. Peter Nelson is closely involved with the training of environmental assessors and senior professionals from governments in developing countries. Land Use Consultants are Members of the Institute of Environmental Assessment. For details contact Peter Nelson at Land Use Consultants, 14 Great George Street, Bristol BS1 5RH, UK (e-mail: admin@Bristol.landuse.co.uk; tel:(+44) 0117 929 1997).

The development of PACE was funded by the RSPB and EN. For further information and recent developments contact Mark Robins, Senior Conservation Officer at RSPB South West England Office, Keble House, Southernhay Gardens, Exeter, EX1 1NT (e-mail: mark.robins@rspb.org.uk tel:(+44) 01392 432691).

References

Burr, S.W. (1995) Sustainable tourism development and use: Follies, foibles, and practical approaches. In S.F. McCool (ed.) *Linking Tourism, the Environment, and Sustainability: Setting the Stage* (pp. 8–13). Washington, DC: US Department of Agriculture Technical Report INT-GTR-323.

Christensen, N.A. (1995) Sustainable community based tourism and host quality of life. In S.F. McCool (ed.) *Linking Tourism, the Environment, and Sustainability: Setting the Stage* (pp. 63–8). Washington, DC: US Department of Agriculture Technical Report INT-GTR-323.

Department of Employment (1989) *Environmental Assessment – A Guide to the Procedures.* London: HMSO.

EEC (1985) *European Council Directive, 85/337/EEC.*

EU (1996) *Council Directive 96/0304(syn).*

Getz, D. and Jamal, T.B. (1994) The environment–community symbiosis: A case for collaborative planning. *Journal of Sustainable Tourism* 2 (3), 152–73.

Halcrow-Fox (1992) *Brue Valley Feasibility Study Phase 1.* Somerset County Council.

Hughes, G. (1995) Cultural construction of sustainable tourism. *Tourism Management* 16 (1), 49–59.

Hunter, C.J. (1995) On the need to re-conceptualise sustainable tourism development. *Journal of Sustainable Tourism* 3 (3), 165.

IUCN (1995) Assessing rural sustainability – 25 steps, Draft Booklet, Monitoring and Assessing Progress Towards Sustainability Project. World Conservation Union.

Knowles-Lankford, J. and Lankford, S.V. (1995) Sustainable practices: Implications for tourism recreation development. In S.F. McCool (ed.) *Linking Tourism, the Environment, and Sustainability: Setting the Stage* (pp. 18–22). Washington, DC: US Department of Agriculture Technical Report INT-GTR-323.

Land Use Consultants (1994) *Brue Valley Feasibility Study Phase 2, Avalon Marshes – Discussion of Options & Topic Reports.*

Lane, B. (1994) What is rural tourism? *Journal of Sustainable Tourism* 2 (1&2), 7–21.

Macgillivray, A. and Zadek, S. (1995) *Accounting for Change: Indicators for Sustainable Development.* New Economics Foundation.

Runyan, D. (1977) Tools for community-managed impact assessment. *Journal of American Institute of Planners* 43, 125–34.

Somerset County Council (1992) *Peat Local Plan.* Taunton: Somerset County Council.

Somerset County Council. *Avalon Mashes, Creating a Living Asset for Somerset.* Taunton: Somerset County Council.

Slee, B., Farr, P. and Snowden, P. (1996a) Sustainable tourism and the local economy. In *Sustainable Tourism, Ethics and the Environment*, Conference Proceedings, Newton Rigg.

Slee, B., Farr, P. and Snowden, P. (1996b) Tourism strategies and rural development. *Zemedelska Ekonomika* 42 (1), 19–28.

Sutherland, P. and Nicholson, A. (1996) *Wetland Life in the Somerset Levels.* London: Michael Joseph.

Taylor, D. (1997) Avalon's new wetlands. *Enact* 5 (2), 16–19.

Town and County Planning Regulations (1988) *Town & Country Planning (Assessment of Environmental Effects) Regulations.* London: HMSO.

World Commission on Environment and Development (1987) *The Brundtland Report.* Oxford: Oxford University Press.

Chapter 3

Peripheries, Artificial Peripheries and Centres

JULIE SCOTT

To talk of *peripheral regions* is to invoke a relationship, for peripheries only are peripheries in relation to other places designated *centres*. That relationship is the focus for this paper, which starts with the assumption that *periphery* and *centre* are not fixed, but dynamic categories, expressive of shifting political, economic and symbolic alignments. As tourist products they can be constructed, packaged and marketed to take various forms and fulfil various functions. My aim is to explore that process of construction with particular reference to the case of Northern Cyprus. Cyprus' peripheral position at the easternmost end of the Mediterranean has, paradoxically, tended to put it at the centre of contending regional and global forces, and the present-day political isolation of Northern Cyprus runs counter to a history of connectedness within a network of regional centres. Today, as an unrecognised country wholly dependent on Turkey, Northern Cyprus offers an extreme and illuminating example of a tourism periphery and of the fluidity of categories of periphery and centre.

Centre–periphery relations here refer to relationships between, on the one hand, urban industrial or post-industrial centres and, on the other hand, the tourist destinations: the former, home not only to the world's tourists but also to the commercial, political and economic interests which control the industry; the latter, situated at some distance away from the metropolitan centres and thus cut off from the hubs of power and influence, servicing their leisure and recreation needs. It is a relationship characterised by the power of the centre both to determine events and conditions in the periphery, and to construct the periphery as the object of the metropolitan imagination – that *pleasure periphery* in which the fantasy realm finds its physical location. This has produced a pattern of mass tourism developments concentrated on the attractions of sun, sea, sand and sex, which is now widely criticised as being environmentally, socially and culturally unsustainable. Meanwhile, the market has moved on. Demand is growing for a different kind of tourism product offered by more remote peripheries which exercise a special appeal, in the form of 'unspoilt' landscapes and/or 'traditional' cultures where tourists may experience 'the authentic' (see MacCannell, 1976; Urry, 1995).

Increasingly, mature and declining tourist centres within the 'pleasure periphery' are promoting their own peripheral regions as an alternative to sun, sea and sand tourism (see Morgan, 1994). Nowadays, for example, Majorca's mountain villages, wildlife and nature reserves are being marketed as alternatives to the resorts of Arenal, Palma Nova and Magaluf; government brochures treat tourists in Malta to a much more sophisticated review of the culture of the island than was the case in the past, and tourists are encouraged to attend the *festi* which are a traditional and colourful part of village life (Morgan, 1994; Boissevain, 1996a). The villages of Majorca and Malta do not have to be inaccessible or even particularly far-flung to exercise the appeal of 'the periphery'. Indeed, in the case of hill-tribe trekking in Thailand, Cohen has shown how modes of travel and markers of the remote and exotic can be manipulated in order to create the desired effect (Cohen, 1989). Peripheries are being constructed and marketed – and increasingly so, as a means to spread the tourist dollar, revive a jaded tourism product and relieve the pressures on coastal areas.

This process can even be observed in the product placement of destinations whose credentials as a periphery seem self-evident. The case of Dominica, an island in the eastern Caribbean, offers an interesting example. Unable to compete with the sun, sea and sand tourism offered by other Caribbean islands because of its unfavourable eastern location, vulnerability to hurricanes, and absence of white-sand beaches, Dominica's marketing strategy capitalised on its differences from other Caribbean islands by promoting itself as a regional centre for 'Alternative Tourism', an island of '365 rivers', in contrast to Antigua's boast of '365 beaches' (Weaver, 1991).[1] The obstacles of geographical isolation and inaccessibility can, therefore, produce a high-quality tourism product, and be turned to good marketing account, one reason why tourism is seen as the only development option in some places.

However, peripheral regions are then faced with a paradox, for if the appeal of peripheries is, as Urry (1995) argues, based on their power to signify to the visitor the unspoilt, the pristine, the traditional – in contrast to the symbolic associations of the centre (and increasingly of mass tourism resorts in the pleasure periphery) with the inauthentic, the spoilt, the jaded, the modern – then tourism development itself can destroy the basis of the place's appeal (Urry, 1995). In this sense, Selwyn suggests, peripheral regions are essentially mythical places, dependent on their continued marginalisation in order to sustain the power of the myth (Selwyn, 1996: 1–32; see also Hutt, 1996; Fees, 1996).

What are the trade-offs between tourist image, tourism development and sustainability in peripheral regions, and who sets the terms of those trade-offs? I turn to the case of Northern Cyprus in order to explore some possible answers. Northern Cyprus, I suggest, can be considered an *artificial periphery*, which actually functions as several different kinds of periphery at once. I consider how these functions affect the Northern Cyprus product, the implications of this for local aspirations and development options, and how these fit with the present political situation and likely future scenarios for Cyprus.

Northern Cyprus

Since the partition of Cyprus in 1974, the diplomatic, economic and cultural boycotts imposed on the North by the international community have resulted in enforced dependence on Turkey and relative isolation from the rest of the world.[2] A civil aviation boycott on direct flights to Northern Cyprus means that access to the North is mediated via Turkey or, at the internal border between northern and southern parts of the island, by the Republic of Cyprus government of the south.[3] Journey times from London to the North's Ercan Airport are normally six or seven hours compared with four hours to Larnaca in the south, and fare prices are also correspondingly higher. Northern Cyprus can, therefore, be considered an artificial periphery, receiving 385,759 foreign visitors in 1995, compared with 2.1 million in the Republic of Cyprus and 7.7 million in Turkey, which are now well-established tourism centres.[4]

Dependent development

Since 1974, tourism in Northern Cyprus has suffered from surplus bed capacity, with occupancy rates rarely exceeding 35% (Lockhart and Ashton, 1990). However, at New Year, and the religious Bayram holidays, there are not enough beds to cope with the demand from Turkish tourists. While the south of the island also depends heavily on one major market (the British market, which makes up about 40% of total arrivals), the North's dependence on the single market of Turkey is much higher, at about 75% of total arrivals. Expatriate Turkish Cypriots, and older, middle-class British and German tourists, make up the bulk of other arrivals. Turkey is the major gateway market, and also a competitor for Northern Cyprus. Tourism development in Northern Cyprus is, therefore, peculiarly contingent on developments in Turkey, as the following brief summary of recent trends illustrates.

Turkish tourism to Cyprus during the 1980s was based on 'luggage tourism' – shopping trips of only one or two days' duration, staying in cheap and often unregistered accommodation, to take advantage of price and custom tariff differentials by buying large quantities of retail goods on commission for resale in Turkey. During the mid 1980s, a new economic strategy was announced. Tourism was declared the leading sector of the economy, with the lion's share of resources – largely in the form of incentive credits from Turkey – being earmarked for assistance to tourism development, at the expense of other sectors, especially agriculture. The policy aimed to reduce the reliance on the luggage tourism trade, and increase the proportion of non-Turkish tourists. This policy, however, met with only limited success, as the statistics in Table 3.1 indicate, and a more recent strategy has been to develop those sectors which appeal specifically to the Turkish market. Thus, when the Islamic Welfare Party (Refah) made moves to reintroduce a ban on Turkish citizens gambling in casinos in Turkey, 17 casinos opened in Northern Cyprus to meet the demand from Turkey for gambling tourism. Meeting the Turkish demand for higher education has proved another lucrative area for Northern Cyprus. At present six universities operate in the north catering to more than 15,000 students from Northern Cyprus, Turkey, Asia and the Middle East. The overwhelming majority of the students are from Turkey, and this has further spin-offs in terms of holidays spent by visiting parents and relatives (Katircioglu and Bicak, 1996).

Table 3.1 Number and origin of tourists

Country		Turkey	Other	Total
1991	No.	179,379	40,858	220,237
	% share	81.4	18.6	100.0
1992	No.	210,178	57,440	267,618
	% share	78.5	21.5	100.0
1993	No.	281,370	77,943	359,313
	% share	78.3	21.7	100.0
1994	No.	256,549	95,079	351,628
	% share	73.0	27.0	100.0
1995	No.	298,026	87,773	385,759
	% share	77.3	22.7	100.0

Source: TRNC State Planning Office

In the absence of major foreign companies willing to invest under the present political circumstances, Northern Cyprus' tourism relies heavily on Turkish investment as well as Turkish tourists. High interest rates and high inflation imported from the Turkish economy, combined with uncertainty about the future, are major problems, and while aid packages from Turkey provide for incentive credit at subsidised interest rates, most would-be local investors are put off by the short pay-back time allowed. Most of the very few large hotels in Northern Cyprus are pre-1974 constructions built by Greek Cypriot and foreign investors. Those which are not in the closed district of Varosha (the Greek Cypriot suburb of Famagusta,

since 1974 abandoned and under Turkish military control, in which most of
the pre-1974 development was concentrated) were leased by the Turkish
Cypriot authorities to local and mainland managers. Over the past 15 years
the number of tourist beds has increased from 3782 to 7453, and these have
been in small– to medium-size hotels, holiday villages and self-catering
apartments. The current construction boom in Northern Cyprus reflects the
demand for student accommodation, and London-based Turkish Cypriots
building villas for their retirement or summer houses.

High leakages, compounded by the level of imports of agricultural
produce from Turkey, are a major and growing problem for the local
economy. The consolidation of Northern Cyprus' dependence on the
Turkish tourist market has been accompanied by increasing dependence
on Turkish investment and a concentration of control of the local tourist
industry in Turkish ownership. One reason for this is the change in the
Turkish market now coming to Cyprus. Luggage tourism has dwindled
compared with its significance in former years, thanks to the liberalisation
of import restrictions and tax duties in Turkey. The Turkish tourists now
coming to Northern Cyprus are both more affluent and more diverse than
previously. Within the past few years major Turkish companies have
acquired hotels and the lease of tourist facilities in Northern Cyprus, and
nearly all the new casinos are owned by mainland companies. These big
companies are better resourced than local Turkish Cypriot businesses, and
also have close links with the Turkish market which is the major user of
these facilities. Widespread concern at the limited nature of local control
has been aired in the course of a public controversy over the control of the
national carrier Cyprus Turkish Airlines.[5]

Certainly Northern Cyprus' tourism exhibits a pattern of dependent
development common in peripheral regions, and particularly reminiscent
of the relationship between Swaziland and South Africa documented by
Harrison (1995). Indeed, North Cyprus, like Swaziland, is doubly peripheral because the regional centre on which it depends is itself a periphery.
Northern Cyprus' development is, therefore, manifestly held back in many
ways by its status as a periphery. The question I now turn to is what, if
anything, does it *gain* from its peripheral status?

Central and peripheral attractions

Northern Cyprus' isolation has had both positive and negative consequences in terms of its image and marketing. On the negative side,
commercially available maps of Cyprus show the north as an area under
military occupation and hence inaccessible and potentially dangerous.
Many travel agents in the UK are unaware of its tourism or even of its existence. On the other hand, having missed out on the rapid tourism development of the rest of the region, Northern Cyprus is in the position to offer
certain unique features as 'unspoilt Northern Cyprus; ... the only

remaining unspoilt corner of the Mediterranean; tranquil Northern Cyprus
... one of Europe's last unspoilt hideaways'.[6] The traditional Mediterranean rural landscape, which has evolved over thousands of years, is still
pervasive throughout the north, its flora and fauna extremely rich and
diverse, and including several rare and endangered species (Makhzoumi,
1996). Marketing slogans such as 'a corner of earth touched by heaven'
emphasise both Northern Cyprus' peripherality and the paradisical nature
of that periphery.

But, I suggest, in terms of its symbolic appeal, Northern Cyprus functions as at least three different kinds of periphery, each of which appeals to
a particular segment of its tourist market.

First, Northern Cyprus functions as a kind of education and pleasure
periphery for the Turkish market. Apart from its universities, the North's
main attractions for this market are a combination of sun, sea and sand,
shopping and the opportunity for casino gambling. For Turkish tourists,
who find similarities with the language, religion, customs and even antiq-
uities of the mainland, Northern Cyprus is perhaps not different enough to
function as a cultural tourism periphery. Local handicrafts, for example, do
not sell well to Turkish tourists, who prefer to shop for toiletries, cosmetics
and designer label fashion wear. Daily tours which are organised for
Turkish and other foreign tourists by hotels and travel agencies show fasci-
nating variations which reveal much about how Northern Cyprus is
constructed for different audiences. Shopping stops, for example, are a
regular feature of Turkish tours, as are visits to landmarks and memorials
of the 1974 military intervention. One Turkish tourist, discussing the differences between tours organised for British, German and Turkish tourists,
suggested that Cyprus holds the same significance for many Turkish visitors as the Normandy landing beaches for the British. For some Turkish
tourists, then, there is an element of pilgrimage in a visit to Cyprus.[7]

There is pilgrimage, too, but of a different kind, for the expatriate
Turkish Cypriot market, for whom the trip back to Cyprus represents an
annual pilgrimage 'home'.[8] Many overseas-based Cypriots return in the
summer to celebrate their weddings and circumcisions, and buy gold and
foodstuffs which represent home to them: locally produced olive oil and
hellim cheese; dried *tarhana* and *molahiya*. Although few invest in businesses
in Northern Cyprus, they are an important stimulus to the construction
industry and land and property market, as they build villas for retirement
and for holiday homes.

Northern Cyprus' third peripheral manifestation is as a nature/culture
periphery for a Northern European market seeking, as the North's
marketing slogan has it, 'a corner of earth touched by heaven' in the Mediterranean. Northern Cyprus appeals both to the myths of northern European tourists about the Mediterranean '*Other*', and to a sense of nostalgia
for qualities which many tourists feel have been lost in their own societies.[9]

The villages of the Kyrenia range of mountains provide ample reminders of the pre-independence Cyprus made famous in Lawrence Durrell's book *Bitter Lemons*, and foreign tourists frequently comment on the beauty of the landscape, the peace and quiet, the sense of safety, and 'traditional' Mediterranean friendliness and hospitality as features of the lack of commercialism. Special interest tours such as walking and painting holidays, archaeology and botanical tours are a feature of this market.

... and the locals?

Northern Cyprus may market itself as a desirable periphery, but the other aspects of being a periphery – the problem of its dependent development and the limitations this imposes – are also painfully clear to Turkish Cypriots. High inflation, low wages and lack of economic opportunities, particularly for the young educated, are chronic problems. Tourism's performance as the leading sector of the economy has been disappointing. In 1995 it contributed 3.3% of GDP, but given the high level of leakages, the tourism multiplier is estimated to be low.[10] Tourist numbers remain stagnant, and the continuing international political impasse over Cyprus, combined with periodic border incidents and the threat of further military action, make the prospects of tapping into the highly price- and security-sensitive European sun-lust market extremely doubtful. Nevertheless, tourism policy so far has concentrated on efforts to increase bed capacity and investment in the accommodation sector, and on the issue of price competitiveness with southern Cyprus and Turkey, rather than on serious attempts to capitalise on the north's unique attractions by developing sustainable low-impact, high-quality tourism. In 1998 the policy objective of raising bed capacity to 25,000 (a 200% increase) and annual tourist arrivals to 750,000 (a 100% increase) within five years was declared.[11]

In pursuing this option, it seems that it is actually the North's peripheral status which is being rejected: Northern Cyprus is not a periphery, but a tourist centre in waiting. The cultural, political and economic grounds for this stance have a long provenance. Cyprus has a millennia-long tradition as the crossroads of east and west: at the centre of struggles between the Latin and Eastern Orthodox Christian rites, as the last bastion of the Crusaders against Islam, and as a strategic base for global and regional powers. Thanks to Cyprus' position at the centre of ancient sea-trading routes, its merchants achieved enormous prosperity, with Famagusta amongst the most spectacularly wealthy cities of the Middle Ages. During the 20th century, Turkish Cypriot migration has created a global diaspora, and families in Northern Cyprus have members spread throughout the world's great urban centres. Rejection of the status of periphery is, in part, an assertion of these historic connections, and an affirmation of faith in the future, reflecting the hope or expectation that a solution to 'the Cyprus Problem' will one day be found.

The Turkish Cypriot sense of belonging to the major currents of the world, rather than an isolated backwater, does not find a resonance with their present main markets, as the following headline from a major colour feature in the travel pages of a British Sunday quality paper illustrates:

> Economic isolation is the north's main attraction. It is one of the few places in the Mediterranean untainted by development. (Balmer, 1998)

For many Turkish Cypriots, the cost of maintaining this idyll for British tourists is too high. At the same time, the Turkish market also poses some problems of self-image. In part these date back to the heyday of the luggage tourists, whose image still dominates Turkish Cypriot notions of Turkish tourists. Despite the changes in the Turkish market referred to earlier, Ministry of Tourism statistics for 1995 show that Turkish tourists, who made up 77.3% of arrivals, accounted for only 48% of hotel guests and 35% of all bednights, whereas all other nationalities accounted for 22.7%, 52% and 65% respectively. Turkish tourists simply do not conform to Turkish Cypriot ideas of 'proper tourism'. If present tourism policies focus on price competitiveness with Turkey and southern Cyprus as models of successful tourism development, I suggest that this is not only because of their greater prosperity, but also because they represent 'proper' tourism, with the associations of legitimacy and place in the mainstream which that connotes.

Research by Akis *et al.* (1996) on resident attitudes to tourism of both Greek and Turkish Cypriots showed that Turkish Cypriot respondents had a generally positive attitude towards tourism development, tempered with a degree of caution concerning possible future impacts indicated by a high proportion of neutral or don't know responses.[12] The examples of southern Cyprus and Turkey are, again, relevant here, for as well as being considered tourism success stories, they are known to Turkish Cypriots in terms of the damage mainstream mass tourism development can inflict. The tourism industry has already started to introduce a pattern of internal tourist centres and peripheries. Most tourism investment is concentrated in the Kyrenia region, where two of the island's six universities are based, and which has become the focus of domestic weekend tourism and nightlife. Famagusta, where the biggest university is located, has also seen major growth. Both places are now experiencing many of the problems of Mediterranean tourism centres, including conflict and competition over extremely limited water resources, municipal authorities unable to meet the growing demand for infrastructure, coastal-strip development and commercial exploitation of beaches which restrict local access. However, most other parts of the north remain largely untouched.

The dilemma and challenge for Turkish Cypriot tourism is how to reconcile the desire to be a centre again – including a tourist centre, with its associated pressures and problems – with a growing environmental awareness. Turkish Cypriots frequently criticise the *betonlasma* – the concreting over –

of southern Cyprus and Turkey and, gradually, of some parts of northern Cyprus. This point of view reflects both the awareness that Northern Cyprus has something different to offer, and increasing concern with environmental issues which is also indicated by the rising local membership of organisations such as Greenpeace, Friends of the Earth and societies for the protection of birds and marine life. Young Cypriots, in particular, see the preservation of unique aspects of Turkish Cypriot culture and landscape as important, in terms both of their own heritage and as a valuable tourism resource. As the problems of some of the tourist centres become apparent, and as people increasingly forsake villages and farming for urban occupations, attention is starting to be focused on the future of North Cyprus' internal peripheries, and in particular its most dramatic periphery, the Karpas peninsula.

Cyprus in a Nutshell: The Karpas Peninsula

There are not many tours in Northern Cyprus which require as much careful preparation as a visit to the Karpaz area, where one has to decide in advance, what to see. One should also have enough petrol, as the only large petrol station in the Karpaz is at Yenierenkoy. (Berner, undated)

A narrow peninsula about 72 km long from east to west, the Karpas peninsula dramatically encapsulates the properties of peripherality in all its aspects, and is often referred to by visitors and travel-writers as 'another world' where the rhythm of life is completely different. Its very shape – almost cut off from the rest of Cyprus and extending half way to Syria – makes it extraordinary. It is extraordinary in a number of other ways too: for the sheer quantity and variety of its flora and fauna, which include many rare and endangered species; for its feral animal population, including, most spectacularly, the herds of donkeys which can be seen grazing towards dusk; for its tracts of uncultivated land and sweeping empty beaches where turtles nest; for the pilgrimage centre of St Andrew, situated almost at the tip of the peninsula, where miracles of healing are said to be worked; and for its numerous sites of antiquity which, devoid of the packaging of heritage or interpretation, seem to await constant fresh discovery. Karpas has all the ingredients for a voyage of discovery, and visitors following the advice from the guidebook quoted earlier, and the other sensible hints (to take a long pair of trousers and a torch, and to leave a note in the hotel saying where you are going) may well have a sense of being intrepid travellers rather than tourists.

The history of the Karpas demonstrates well the fluidity of categories of periphery and centre. In ancient times, when boats navigated by keeping land in sight as far as possible, the eastern cape of Karpas, which is only 60 miles from Syria, was the first landmark of Cyprus, and boats sailed up and down the long Karpas coastline, calling in at the numerous little harbours which were still in use for collecting agricultural produce until as recently as the 1930s, when they became unusable by the more modern, larger-draught craft (Hanworth, no date). There is evidence that the mediaeval population of the Karpas region was much larger than its present population of about 12,000 spread over 26 small, scattered settlements. For 300 years the easternmost village of Dipkarpaz (Rizo Karpaso) was the seat of the Orthodox Archbishop of Cyprus. Karpas' present status as a periphery is, to a great extent, the result of a shift away from the old outward-looking maritime links with the region, towards inland centres of power and authority and the concomitant reliance on land-based transport along the one main winding road to the regional centre of Famagusta.

Undoubtedly, however, it has also been caused by post-1974 social and demographic upheavals and the impact of Northern Cyprus' political and economic isolation. The majority of the Greek Cypriot population left Karpas and went south after 1974, and the area has been largely resettled by Turkish mainland settlers, a number of whom are themselves Greek-speakers from the Black Sea region. The main occupations of the region are agriculture and animal husbandry, and both are in serious difficulties. The drought which has afflicted Northern Cyprus since 1993 has also affected the Karpas region, and in the easternmost part these effects have been exacerbated by the depredations of the feral animals, whose grazing has also suffered from the lack of water. Problems in marketing agricultural produce have also affected the local economy. Tobacco production, which used to be a mainstay of the region, has dropped from 122 tons in 1989 to 1 ton in 1994, and the tobacco factories in Dipkarpaz (Rizo Karpaso) and Yeni Erenkoy (Yialousa) stand idle (Statistical Year Book, 1995). Attempts to establish viniculture in the region have also failed, and a new wine factory built in Mehmetcik (Galatya) has never been used. Animal husbandry has also been hit by the fall in livestock prices.

Yet in some senses, Karpas is not a periphery. Its image, of long empty beaches and typical Mediterranean maquis landscape, is central to the image Northern Cyprus promotes of itself as a whole, and these images of Karpas feature in the North's tourism posters and publicity. The Karpas can be said to encapsulate the 'essential experience' of Northern Cyprus, as the following extracts from the publicity for a day trip to Karpas, advertised on the noticeboard of a hotel reception near Kyrenia, illustrate:

> *The Undiscovered Land*: Come with us to the Karpas peninsula and discover the undiscovered! The Karpas peninsula is known as the panhandle of Cyprus and represents North Cyprus in a nutshell. Time here has completely stood still. We wend our way through North Cyprus's most remote villages – home to warm-hearted people, both Greek and Turkish Cypriot – mile upon mile of unspoilt beaches, and

spectacular scenery ... Meet Greek Cypriot, Turkish Cypriot and mainland Turkish living in harmony, side by side. Visit their mosques and
churches, and see the traditional crops – olives, tobacco and cotton.
Sample true Cypriot hospitality over lunch with a difference – typical
village cuisine – something that cannot be found in the restaurants of
Kyrenia and Famagusta. Wild donkeys, history and magic at St
Andrews monastry, where pilgrims come from far and wide to take the
healing waters and fashion wax effigies as an aid to their prayers for the
sick ...

The denial of history to a region which has actually undergone many
changes over the centuries and indeed been transformed over the past few
decades is a striking example of what Fabian (1983) has called the *'denial of
coevalness'*, a rhetorical device by which the Other is both constructed and
objectified. There may, indeed, be something of this in the special status the
Karpas holds in the eyes of many Turkish Cypriots, although in that case it
is also an aspect of the Self which is being objectified – or idealised. Yet to
dismiss the previous passage entirely would be to fail to recognise the
special status of the Karpas, which exists beyond the rhetoric employed.
The picture of the Karpas painted here is that of a liminal space – a space
outside everyday reality, where normal rules and routines are suspended.
This is the logic of pilgrimage. To penetrate to the sacred centre situated at
the extreme limits of the periphery is to penetrate to the essence, to an inner
core of meaning which is both the reward and culmination of the journey. It
is no accident that the sacred centre of St Andrew's monastery, revered and
used by both Turkish and Greek Cypriots, is located at the most remote
extreme of this periphery, since its power is both drawn from and, in turn,
conferred on its peripheral location.

The iconic status of the Karpas peninsula is, I would suggest, strengthened rather than weakened by the fact that it is the locus for several
cross-cutting and often contradictory layers of meaning. In many ways it
captures the deep-seated ambivalence which runs through Turkish
Cypriot attitudes to the past, and to the split *Turkish* and *Cypriot* components of their identity, combining both a Greek Cypriot presence which is
no longer perceived as threatening, and a large Turkish settler presence
which is deeply unpopular in some sections of Turkish Cypriot society.
Turkish Cypriot attitudes to the Karpas Greeks combine surveillance and
control at the official level, with a generally well-disposed interest and
concern on the part of ordinary Turkish Cypriots. In the summer of 1998 the
revival of the children's folk festival organised by the teachers at the Greek
Cypriot primary school in Dipkarpas was featured in the daily paper *Kibris*
with front-page colour photographs and reports that it had been attended
by many Turkish Cypriots (*Kibris*, 1998). The Turkish mainland settlers in
Karpas, meanwhile, have arguably become the keepers of the Turkish

Karpas tradition on behalf of Turkish Cypriots, for while Turkish Cypriot villages have an ageing and declining population, thanks to steady out-migration either to the towns of Northern Cyprus or abroad, farming and handicraft production is kept alive largely by the Turkish settlers from the poorest parts of rural Turkey, many of whom, as mentioned earlier, also maintain the tradition of bilingualism. Thus it falls to the Turkish settlers in Karpas to embody tradition both in its positively valued aspect, but also as negatively valued backwardness from which Turkish Cypriots prefer to distance themselves.[13] In embracing all these references and fundamental points of ambivalence, Karpas functions at the level of the *'condensed symbol'* which, according to Turner and Turner (1978), is the hallmark of the most powerful pilgrimage places.

Karpas remains a central cultural reference for Turkish Cypriots, including those who seldom go there. It also has potential as a regional conservation centre because of the number of rare and endangered varieties of plant, bird, animal and marine life to be found there (Warner, 1997). After years of organisation and lobbying by the National Trust of North Cyprus, a coalition of expatriate residents and Turkish Cypriots, in 1998 the legislation for the establishment of a National Park was finally enacted, extending eastwards from a point west of Dipkarpaz to cover some 155 km². An ambitious alternative proposal, seeking to expand the area within the National Park and incorporate a community development programme in Dipkarpaz village, with sustainable village tourism which would use renovated village houses and prohibit touristic construction, has not been adopted (Yuksel, 1996).

Opening up the Karpas Peninsula

It is in this context that the current road improvement project should be viewed, which is widening and straightening the road from Famagusta all the way to Dipkarpaz. Karpas, with its beautiful coastline and sweeping empty beaches, is ripe for opening up as a recreational periphery. It is a widely held opinion, frequently expressed to me by Turkish Cypriot friends and neighbours and reiterated during my visit at the *kaymakamlik* – the district office located in Famagusta with responsibility for the Karpas region – that tourism is set shortly to explode in the Karpas, and in the view of many this will bring enormous social and economic benefits to the region. Already the wise words of the guidebook, quoted at the opening of this section, need no longer be heeded, because there are now several modern petrol stations in Karpas. Accommodation provision is also starting to creep up, and the building of at least two beach side holiday villages, each with a bed capacity of several thousand, has already started. A speculative dash for land has begun, headed by the most wealthy and powerful of North Cyprus' elite, and stimulated both by the road construction and by the longstanding proposals for the development of the Karpas for tourists, made by a French mission to Cyprus in the 1960s and widely circulated since then. This assumed that the essential qualities of Karpas could be retained at the same time as a 6000-bed tourist complex was built on its most splendid beach, a few miles from the peninsula's tip (Ministry of Commerce and Industry, Cyprus, and Ministère des Affaires Etrangères, France, 1962; for a recent Turkish Cypriot comment on the plan, see Debes, 1997). Interestingly in view of the present discussion, the plan also proposed opening a direct ferry service from Karpas to Lebanon, which would have restored the historic primacy of the Karpas' regional maritime links.

If the establishment of the National Park is an acknowledgement of Karpas' role as a periphery of central national and regional importance, it is a much reduced periphery, with the National Park's western boundary a bulwark against the changes taking place in the rest of Karpas (the *'park shed'*), and indeed the rest of Northern Cyprus. Ironically, as Mahkzoumi (1996) points out, the creation of a National Park may give the green light to insensitive development elsewhere by prioritising one small area for conservation. Another irony is that the road improvement programme, in fact, emphasises and intensifies the region's dependence on a distant centre, with the likelihood that future developments will be controlled by, and primarily benefit, commercial interests located in the tourist centres – as Boissevain (1996b) has documented in the case of Mdina in Malta.

Conclusion

The Karpas region seems to encapsulate on a micro-level the problems and dilemmas of the peripherality of Northern Cyprus as a whole. Isolation may have provided protection so far from the worst aspects of uncontrolled tourism development. However, on a Mediterranean island whose landscape is the outcome of thousands of years of human cultivation and activity, the corollary of lack of development is not necessarily preservation, but neglect and decay – and these are becoming as obtrusive in some areas of Northern Cyprus as the beginnings of inappropriate tourism development are in others.

Tourism development is now underway, and standing still is no longer an option. With this reality in mind, a report by the University of North London commissioned as part of the work on a tourism master plan for Northern Cyprus recommends a strategy of *'niche plus'* tourism development, which would combine optimising the use of existing beach-focused accommodation with developing low-impact, high-quality special interest nature, culture- and activity-based tourism (Selwyn, 1998). One advantage of such a strategy is that the development of the tourist product, in its widest sense, would require the strengthening of local linkages and support for local activities, thus securing local development and reducing dependence on external centres.

The future for Northern Cyprus, and Karpas, as a tourist destination ultimately depends, however, on the political future of Cyprus. With the current stalemate over membership of the European Union for Cyprus and Turkey, the declared intention of the north is to intensify and formalise integration with Turkey. If, on the other hand, a political settlement with the south is achieved, then the floodgates will be opened to the major conventional mass tour operators. The question is no longer will there be tourism development or not, but what kind of tourism development will there be, and what kind of periphery will Northern Cyprus become as a result – another large-scale Mediterranean pleasure periphery, providing short-term profits for international tour operators and local/regional elites, or an environment where small-scale development can flourish and a sustainable future be created, based on the full range of Cyprus' considerable attractions?

Acknowledgements

My thanks to Tom Selwyn for his comments on an earlier draft of this paper, and also to Ufuk Ozaktanlar, Mine Haktanir and Sahap Asikoglu.

Notes

1. Weaver's contention, that Dominica offered a rare example of a deliberate application of an 'alternative tourism' strategy to a whole country, was questioned in a later rejoinder by Oppermann and Sahr (1992) who argued that the alternative tourism developments on the island were merely circumstantial. They themselves identified signs of incipient conventional mass tourism in Dominica.
2. It is beyond the scope of this paper to go into all the issues surrounding the intercommunal and global political tensions leading to the collapse of the 1960 independent constitution and the subsequent division of Cyprus. Suffice it to say that events themselves, their interpretation and the language used to refer to them are hotly contested and highly politicised. Since 1974, Greek Cypriots have been living in the southern two-thirds of the island, which is internationally recognised as the Republic of Cyprus, and the northern third has been home to the Turkish Cypriot population. The Turkish Republic of Northern Cyprus, which was unilaterally declared in 1983, is recognised only by Turkey.
3. According to Turkish Cypriot figures collected at the Ledra Palace checkpoint, 33,537 foreigners from the south visited the north in 1995 (Source: Polis Genel Mudurlugu, Nicosia, TRNC).
4. Turkish Republic of Northern Cyprus (TRNC) State Planning Organization, 1997; Republic of Cyprus Department of Statistics and Research/Ministry of Finance, 1995; Republic of Turkey Ministry of Tourism, 1995. The Northern Cyprus figures exclude arrivals of Turkish Cypriot nationals, which, if included, bring the total number of arrivals for 1995 to 520,000 (TRNC Ministry of Tourism, Tourism Statistics 1995).
5. Reports in *Kibris* newspaper, e.g. KTHY Krizi Tirmaniyor, *Kibris* 1997. Cyprus Turkish Airlines is co-owned by Turkish Airlines and the North Cyprus govern-

ment. Although Northern Cyprus owns a majority share in the company, Turkish Airlines has a majority of the representatives on the board.
6. Advertisements for Celebrity Holidays, President Holidays, and Cyprus Paradise in *The Observer* 30 August 1998.
7. On the subject of guided tours in Northern Cyprus see Scott (1995a).
8. Peripheral, in a practical sense, to the everyday life of most expatriate Turkish Cypriots, but retaining a central significance as a cultural and identity reference, Northern Cyprus functions for this market as a kind of '*sacred periphery*'. See Mandel's (1990) analysis of the annual return home to Turkey of Turkish Gastarbeiter from Germany.
9. Selwyn (1996) and letters pages to the English language weekly published in Northern Cyprus, *Cyprus Today*.
10. One estimate puts it at well under a factor of one (Bulunc, 1995).
11. Announced on TV by the Permanent Secretary for Tourism (*Ucuncu Boyut* BRT 24 April 1998).
12. At a conference in Kyrenia in 1995 there was a clear split between Turkish Cypriot participants arguing in favour of mass tourism development, and foreign participants arguing against it. The views of the general public, canvassed in the survey on issues such as social, cultural and economic effects of tourism, environmental impacts, distribution of benefits and effects on the quality of life, showed more caution than those of the industry representatives at the conference.
13. For a discussion of the evolution of the demographic structure of the North, and implications for the future, see Feridun (1998); on the question of Turkish Cypriot markers of modernity and tradition, see Scott (1995b).

References

Akis, S., Peristianis, N. and Warner, J. (1996) Residents' attitudes to tourism development: The case of Cyprus. *Tourism Management* 17 (7), 481–94.
Balmer, D. (1998) Northern Cyprus, *The Observer* (30 August).
Boissevain, J. (1996a) Ritual, tourism and cultural commoditization in Malta. In T. Selwyn (ed.) *The Tourist Image* (pp. 105–20). Chichester: Wiley.
Boissevain, J. (1996b) But we live here! Perspectives on cultural tourism in Malta. In L. Briguglio, R. Butler, D. Harrison and W. L. Filho (eds) *Sustainable Tourism in Islands and Small States: Case Studies* (Island Studies Series). London: Pinter.
Berner, U. (no date) Karpaz: The Panhandle. *Cyprus Letters*, Freiburg.
Bulunc, A.Z. (1995) The significance of the tourism sector in the economic development of TRNC and the Tourism Multiplier. Unpublished MSc thesis, University of the Eastern Mediterranean, Famagusta.
Cohen, E. (1989) Primitive and remote: Hill tribe trekking in Thailand. *Annals of Tourism Research* 16, 30–61.
Debes, T. (1997) Eski Bir Fransiz-Kibris Ortak Yapimi Turizm Master Plani. *Journal for Cypriot Studies* 3 (2), 197–205.
Fabian, J. (1983) *Time and the Other*. New York: Columbia University Press.
Fees, C. (1996) Tourism and the politics of authenticity in a north Cotswold town. In T. Selwyn (ed.) *The Tourist Image*. Chichester: Wiley.
Feridun Feridun (1998) Kuzey Kibris Turk Cumhuriyeti'nin Demografik Yapisi. *Journal for Cyprus Studies* 4 (1), 1–32.
Hanworth, R. (no date) *The Heritage of North Cyprus*. Nicosia: Ministry of Communications, Public Works and Tourism.
Harrison, D. (1995) Development of tourism in Swaziland. *Annals of Tourism Research* 22, 135–56.

Hutt, M. (1996) Looking for Shangri-la: From Hilton to Lamichhane. In T. Selwyn (ed.) *The Tourist Image*. Chichester: Wiley.

Katircioglu, S. and Bicak, H.A. (1996) The economic impact of the overseas students on the North Cyprus Economy. *Journal for Cypriot Studies* 2, 233–66.

Kibris (1997) KTHY Krizi Tirmaniyor (24 July).

Kibris (1998) 'Karpaz'da Rum cocuklarin mutlulugu' (24 June).

Lockhart, D. and Ashton, S. (1990) Tourism to Northern Cyprus. *Geography* 75, 153–67.

MacCannell, D. (1976) *The Tourist*. New York: Schocken.

Makhzoumi, J. M. (1996) The spatial and ecological diversity of regional landscapes as a foundation for regional planning. Unpublished paper presented to the Lefkosa Chapter of the Society for International Development, Lefkosa, 27 November.

Mandel, R. (1990) Shifting centres and emergent identities: Turkey and Germany in the lives of Turkish Gastarbeiter. In D. F. Eickelman and J. Piscatori (eds) *Muslim Travellers. Pilgrimage, Migration and the Religious Imagination*. Berkeley, CA: University of California Press.

Ministry of Commerce and Industry, Cyprus, and Ministère des Affaires Etrangères, France (1962) *Cyprus: Study of Tourist Development*.

Morgan, D. (1994) Homogenous products: The future of established resorts. In W. F. Theobald (ed.) *Global Tourism: The Next Decade*. Oxford: Butterworth-Heinemann.

Oppermann, M. and Sahr (1992) Another view on alternative tourism in Dominica. *Annals of Tourism Research* 19, 784–8.

Republic of Cyprus Department of Statistics and Research/Ministry of Finance (1995) *Tourism, Migration and Travel Statistics*.

Republic of Turkey Ministry of Tourism (1995) *Bulletin of Tourism Statistics*.

Scott, J. (1995a) Identity, visibility and legitimacy in Turkish Cypriot tourism development. Unpublished PhD thesis, University of Kent at Canterbury.

Scott, J. (1995b) Sexual and national boundaries. *Annals of Tourism Research* 22 (2), 385–403.

Selwyn, T. (ed.) (1996) *The Tourist Image*. Chichester: Wiley.

Selwyn, T. (1998) The contribution to the North Cyprus Master Plan prepared by the University of North London's Centre for Leisure and Tourism Studies, Mediterranean Unit.

TRNC Ministry of Tourism (1995) *Tourism Statistics 1995*.

TRNC State Planning Organization (1995) *Statistical Year Book*. Lefkosa.

TRNC State Planning Organization (1997) *Annual Plan 1997*.

Turner, V. and Turner, E. (1978) *Image and Pilgrimage in Christian Culture: Anthropological Perspectives*. Oxford: Blackwell.

Urry, J. (1995) *Consuming Places*. London: Routledge.

Warner, J. (1997) Use value of the Karpas Peninsula. Unpublished Economic Department Discussion Paper, University of the Eastern Mediterranean, Famagusta.

Weaver, D.B. (1991) Alternative to mass tourism in Dominica. *Annals of Tourism Research* 18, 414–32.

Yuksel, D. (1996) Environmentally sustainable management plan for the proposed Karpas Peninsula National Park Area. Unpublished MSc thesis, University of Ankara/Med Campus.

Chapter 4

Tourist Perceptions of the Ultimate European Periphery

JENS KRISTIAN STEEN JACOBSEN

This chapter explores foreign motor tourists' perceptions of North Cape as a tourism destination. North Cape (Nordkapp) is a huge promontory on the top of Europe, on the Norwegian island of Magerøya in the Arctic Ocean. The desolate North Cape is regarded as a symbol of the edge of the (European) world, and has long been a popular attraction for tourists/travellers in Northern Scandinavia. This headland, rising abruptly over 1000 ft (307 m) from the sea, has also been a seamark for more than 1100 years. Today, North Cape appears to be one of the primary elements in the tourist image of Northern Scandinavia. The chapter presupposes that there are several and different perceptions of this site. The focus here is on the perceptions of North Cape both among visitors to this remote locality, and among those motorists from abroad who have not yet visited the site. Utilising data from the Norwegian Foreign Visitor Survey, the chapter presents empirical results of individual motor tourists' perceptions of North Cape.

Background on North Cape

Even though North Cape is regarded as a symbol of the top of Europe, the promontory is, in fact, not the northernmost point of Europe and Magerøya island (see Figure 4.1). But its distinctive form gives this high promontory and established seamark certain advantages over the more northerly but low, insignificant and inaccessible headland of Knivskjellodden (Jacobsen, 1997a). The desolate North Cape has been a fairly popular peripheral destination since the 1870s. To fully understand North Cape's present position as a momentous peripheral attraction, it is necessary to glance briefly back into history. We may surmise that the influence of Romanticism provides the most important background for today's tourism to the alpine landscapes of coastal Norway, where North Cape is situated. Such tourism, influenced by the Romantic movement, is partly explained as a spiritual search for wild landscapes. Norway's mountainous coasts were and still are considered a kind of Alps by the sea (see Ryall & Veiteberg, 1991; Towner, 1985). The growth of interest in both North Cape and Northern Norway in general seems to have coincided with the intrepid

Figure 4.1 Magerøya Island and North Cape

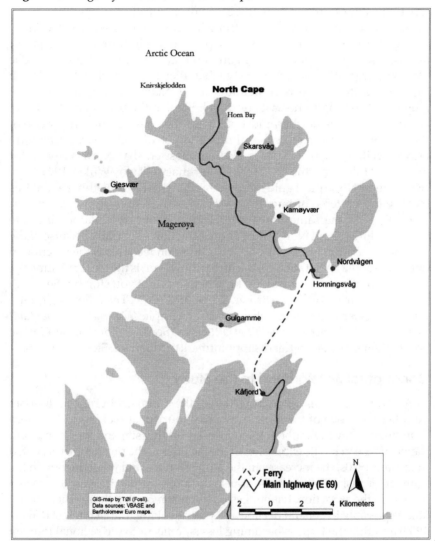

Swedish-Norwegian King Oscar II's visit to the promontory after his coronation in 1873. Thomas Cook's travel bureau in London arranged its first regular tours to North Cape in 1875. And a regular tourist steam ship line to the Cape from Southern Norway was already in operation in 1877. North Cape became accessible to motorists when the present road to the summit was opened in 1956, replacing an 11 km walk from the shore of Horn Bay. The recently expanded facilities, the North Cape Hall, partly cut into the rock of the Cape, include such amenities as a post office, a wrap-around videograph, exhibitions, a souvenir shop and restaurants. Upon the opening of new facilities at the end of the 1980s, the admission fee for visitors to the edge of the plateau increased dramatically.

As a place capable of evoking strong imagery in its observers (Jacobsen, 1997a), North Cape previously took precedence in tourists' selection of attractions in this region. Visitors often remark that this cliff in the Arctic Ocean is larger and more impressive than they had expected. Clark (1994: 313) writes that there is something about North Cape that cannot be laughed off by the iconoclasts of travel. Some guidebooks point out that North Cape, as the northernmost point, is for a considerable proportion of the visitors in this region the ultimate target of their tour, an *idée fixe* (Taylor-Wilkie, 1996: 243). It is also emphasised that North Cape is for many the Holy Grail, the end of their pilgrimage (Taylor-Wilkie, 1994: 343). Even a generally critical guidebook states that there is something about this bleak, wind-battered promontory that excites the senses (Brown & Sinclair, 1993: 321). At the same time, several guidebook presentations indicate mixed feelings about North Cape as an attraction, especially because of the commercialisation of the site and the admission fee. This is the reaction in one guidebook: 'What sticks in the throat, however, is the fee for visiting the Cape, currently a staggering 150 kr, whether or not you stop by the North Cape Hall tourist complex' (Brown & Lee, 1997: 265). The following quotation from a German guidebook is another example: '*Mancher Besucher fühlt sich hier, am Ziel seiner Träume, bitter enttäuscht* (Some visitors feel here, at the goal of their dreams, a bitter disappointment)' (Möbius & Ster, 1994: 120).

Conceptual Background to the Study

As North Cape is often considered the ultimate European tourism periphery and one of the most substantial tourism attractions in Northern Scandinavia, several authors have focused on this site and its visitors as a theme of research. The expansion of the facilities at the promontory initiated in the late 1980s, the increases in the admission fee and the reduction in the number of visitors since 1994 appear to have further increased research interest in the attraction. It is suggested, for instance, that the northern headland is possibly in general decline as a place evoking tourist interest (Viken, 1989) and that the Cape is becoming less significant to the regional tourism industry (Krogh *et al.*, 1996). Jacobsen (1997a) concludes that North Cape, as a travel classic, despite a recent decrease in the number of visitors, will probably have a 'life after death'.

A recent survey among foreign and Norwegian visitors to Northern Scandinavia indicates that tourists' reactions to globalisation and visual commonplaceness are contributing factors in inducing travel to areas that offer distinct experiences of journeying to particular places (Jacobsen, 1993). But a distinct image is not necessarily sufficient to attract demanding visitors. The promotion of place is becoming more important in the tourism industry. And knowledge pertaining to tourists' understanding of important attractions is considered vital to the further development of tourism in a region. As a result of changing tourist interests and increased competition, many places must compete with one another in their endeavours to be included in tourist itineraries. Some destinations have a fragmentary image, indicating that most places are perceived and promoted in different ways to different place 'consumers' (see Ward & Gold, 1994: 11). Because of the expansion of the visual media, individuals may even have quite clear impressions of destinations they have never actually visited. In this chapter, the impression of a place in itself is not the topic, even though the chapter attempts to identify image patterns or tourist perceptions attached to a specific destination. Since it is assumed that there are often changes in impressions of a destination before and after a visit, Echtner and Ritchie (1991: 4) argue that it is desirable to separate the impressions of those who have visited a destination from those who have not. This aspect is given consideration here.

Tourist perceptions of North Cape appear to be influenced by miscellaneous travel interests and different travel style traditions. A survey conducted in the summer season of 1995 shows that some of the most important travel motives for foreign motorists in Northern Norway are to see beautiful scenery, to experience virginal and clean natural surroundings, to enjoy peace and quiet and to travel around and see new places (Jacobsen, 1997b: 31). A search for untamed and intact landscapes is conceivably typical of the tourism in the area. An interest in solitude or, at least, some peace and quiet, appears to be important to a proportion of the visitors. Part of today's travel to Northern Scandinavia is also explained as a component of green tourism. Green tourism, or ecotourism, generally appears to be a result of an increasing interest in the environment and its constituency. This kind of tourism seems to be a variable phenomenon. Krippendorf (1987: 175) suggests that there is an increased interest in returning to simplicity and to nature. Green tourism can be understood as both an escape from everyday life (Tonboe, 1994) and as a protest against modern life and a rejection of the artificial. The green trend also includes communication with vanishing nature and aesthetic or romantic outdoor experiences. In Northern Scandinavia, green tourism is often related to an interest in the local culture and regional way of life, and to the discovery of unique scenery (see Jacobsen, 1993).

Some holiday-makers are of the opinion that the possibilities of experiencing something authentic and typical are dependent on the number of tourists present in an area or at a site, while some people simply dislike the presence of other holiday-makers. Visitors who are susceptible towards crowding at a site and the presence of many fellow travellers are often labelled anti-tourists or travellers (Smith, 1977: 8–11; Aubert, 1965; Pearce, 1982). Anti-tourists are here conceived of as tourists/ travellers who dislike being regarded as ordinary or typical tourists, attempting to distance themselves from the tourist role. According to Pearce, travellers demarcate themselves from tourists by experiments with local food and by exploring new places privately (Pearce, 1982: 32). A cognate discrimination is established by Urry (1990), who distinguishes between the romantic gaze and the collective gaze. The collective tourist gaze takes place in the presence of large numbers of people. The romantic gaze represents some parallels to anti-tourist or traveller attitudes. The typical object of the romantic gaze is undisturbed natural beauty (Urry, 1990: 45). Thirud (1994: 25) suggests that such terms should, in many instances, be used as relative notions, and further points out that a considerable proportion of the landscape tourism to Norway should be characterised as relatively romantic.

An empirical study of visitors to a place somewhat similar to North Cape, the promontory Land's End in England, has shown that crowding and a large number of visitors may degrade the quality of the experience of a site for some visitors (Ireland, 1990). This may be the case for North Cape as well. In this study, it is presumed that there could be somewhat similar differences between motorists of a romantic or a collective bent in terms of how they react to fellow travellers and to the commercial aspects of the Cape. Whether or not North Cape is regarded as undisturbed is, to some extent, dependent on the visitor. Because of the great tourist interest in watching the Midnight Sun from the north-facing plateau high above the Arctic Ocean, some crowding at the headland at midnight is inevitable during the long polar summer day, which lasts from the middle of May until the end of July.

On the one hand, North Cape appears to be a kind of primary (or secondary) attraction (see Leiper, 1990) for many visitors in Northern Scandinavia, conceivably a place one is more or less obliged to visit (see Jacobsen *et al.*, 1998: 119). But on the other hand, the large numbers of visitors and the commercialisation of the site may prevent some tourists from going to the very far North, and possibly also give a proportion of visitors feelings of dissonance when arriving there at the end of their tour.

In summary, there appear to be at least two general and momentous images of North Cape. One is an impression of the Cape as a remote, monumental and impressive place – a sacred site and a symbol of the edge of Europe – to a large extent a product of the heritage of romanticism and the cultivation of dramatic and wild landscapes. The other major image seems to be the idea of this northerly promontory as a touristy place, commercially exploited and altogether crowded, at least around midnight in the high season. One focus of the present research is to detect particular aspects associated with North Cape among all foreign motorists who visited Norway in the summer of 1996. The chapter also aims to recognise some of the main reasons and patterns of reasons for not going to the Cape among those motorists who did not visit this site. The objective of the study was not to construct *a priori* typologies in relation to the tourist impressions of North Cape but rather to unveil potential hidden image structures or perception structures with the help of factor analysis, a multivariate statistical procedure.

The Survey and the Questionnaire

The data applied in this chapter are derived from a survey of foreign motor tourists in Norway in the summer season of 1996. The survey, conducted by the Institute of Transport Economics, involved the registration of and interviews with motor tourists as they exited Norway. Visitor statistics were gathered in various categories. One part involved statistics for holiday visitors staying overnight in Norway (see Haukeland and Rideng, 1997). A questionnaire completed by the respondents included several questions about North Cape. The aspects listed in the questionnaire are derived partly from personal interviews with tourists, and are partly based on previous research (Jacobsen, 1997a; Viken, 1989). The items included in the questionnaire are not assumed to be a complete list of important aspects of North Cape, as foreign tourists regard this attraction. The number of items on the scale of perceptions shown in Tables 4.1 and 4.2 is mainly an outcome of the practical limitations of the questionnaire and the interview time limits in the Norwegian Foreign Visitor Survey. This part of the survey should therefore be considered as a pilot project.

The questionnaire was distributed and collected at nine national highway border crossings and at 11 ferry connections to Sweden, Germany, Denmark and the UK. The questionnaire was available in eight languages: Danish, Dutch, English, Finnish, French, German, Italian and Swedish. The effective sample size was 2482. The response rate was roughly 80%, which was considered fully satisfactory. As with all sample surveys the results are tinged with uncertainty (see Haukeland & Rideng, 1997). About 9% of the respondents visited North Cape in the summer of 1996, while some 10% of the foreign motor tourists had been to this attraction previously. About three out of four respondents answered the question about their interest in or visit to North Cape.

The Factor Analysis

Factor analysis is employed here to identify particular tourists in relation to impressions of specified aspects of North Cape. There are several methods of extracting the factors. In this instance, principal components analysis was employed. With this technique, the total variance of the data is considered. Principal components analysis is considered appropriate when the primary concern is to determine the minimum number of factors that will account for maximum variance in the data. The varimax procedure was used for rotation. This is the most common method of rotation.

The varimax method minimises the number of variables with high loadings on a factor, thereby enhancing the interpretability of the factors (Malhotra, 1993: 627). The rotated factor solutions are presented in Tables 4.3 and 4.4. It is possible to compute as many principal components as there are variables; but, in order to summarise the information contained in the original variables, a small number of factors should be extracted. There are several criteria to determine the number of factors. These include *a priori* determination, approaches based on eigenvalues, scree plot and percentage of variance accounted for. If the number of variables is less than 20, the approach usually results in quite a small number of factors. In these cases, only factors with eigenvalues greater than 1.0 were included, according to a standard procedure. Solutions with other numbers of factors were also tested but they did not appear to be more reasonable in this case.

None of the original eight items of the scale of perceptions of North Cape had low communality (h^2) and no item was excluded for other reasons. Communality is the amount of variance a variable shares with all other variables included in the analysis (Malhotra, 1993: 620). Consequently, the factor analysis was performed on all the items that were included in the questionnaire. Two factors were extracted. The factors concerning tourists' perceptions of North Cape account for 65% of the variance, which is generally regarded as a satisfactory level. The questions concerning reasons for not going to North Cape included a question concerning the importance of previous visits to the promontory. This item had low communality (h^2) and was therefore excluded in the factor analysis. Consequently, the factor analysis was performed on seven of the eight items in the questionnaire. Also in this case, two factors were extracted. These factors account for 60% of the variance, which is here regarded as acceptable.

In the interpretation of the factors, the weight is placed on variables with loadings 0.40 or higher. High loadings indicate a correlation between the variable and the factor. In this investigation, the primary goal of the factor analysis is to reduce the original set of variables to a smaller set of composite variables (factors) for use in subsequent analysis (Malhotra, 1993: 629). For a further interpretation, factor scores for each respondent were calculated. The use of principal components analysis makes it possible to calculate exact factor scores. In principal components analysis, the factor scores are uncorrelated. The standard regression method was chosen to calculate the factor scores. In terms of correlations between the underlying factor and its respective scale, the regression method is considered superior (Kim and Mueller, 1978: 69). In this instance, the definition of a high score is that it is more than 1 or -1. Only the positive scores are utilised in the analysis in this chapter.

The importance of single aspects associated with North Cape

To analyse some important components of the image of North Cape, the Foreign Visitor Survey focused on a selection of destination aspects, mainly general feelings associated with the promontory. With reference to the theoretical framework of Echtner and Ritchie (1991: 5–6), the survey covers both certain attributes of North Cape and some more holistic descriptions of the destination. The foreign motor tourists were asked to state their views regarding the importance of each of eight specific aspects or impressions associated with North Cape. The assumptions of aspects of North Cape mentioned in Table 4.1 served as a basis for the preparation of the questionnaire, in an attempt to find possible patterns of perception among the foreign motorists. The respondents were provided with a rating scale (Likert scale) with four response categories: unimportant, slightly important, fairly important and very important. In the analysis, each statement is assigned a numerical score, ranging from 0 to 3.

The principal aspects of the foreign motor tourists' associations with North Cape are the Midnight Sun, a monumental landscape, impressions of unspoiled scenery and closeness to nature, as shown in Table 4.1. An interest in the experience of a remote part of the world, and the conception of North Cape as Europe's northernmost point are also important. Further, the survey shows that for many of the motor tourists visiting Norway, North Cape is considered a place one should see; the headland is also perceived as a romantic place by a substantial proportion of the motorists.

When compared by how they rate the importance of each aspect of North Cape, those foreign motorists who have visited North Cape differ from

Table 4.1 The importance of aspects associated with North Cape to foreign motor tourists in Norway in the Summer 1996, percentage finding the aspect very important and fairly important

	Visited North Cape in 1996	Visited North Cape on previous trip	Interested in going to North Cape, have not been there	Not interested in North Cape, have not been there	All foreign motorists in Norway 1996
Midnight Sun	85	87	84	59	79
Monumental landscape	89	84	79	54	77
Unspoiled scenery	83	82	81	52	77
Close to nature	76	74	75	50	72
Experience a remote corner of the world	83	76	66	32	64
Europe's northernmost point	85	69	60	31	58
A place one should see	68	64	52	21	51
A romantic place	46	45	43	23	42

others especially in their emphasis of North Cape as a place one should see, in their association of the promontory as Europe's northernmost point, and in their perception of North Cape as a remote part of the world.

The importance of single reasons for not going to North Cape

The foreign motor tourists who did not visit North Cape in the summer season of 1996 were asked to state their views regarding the importance of eight specific reasons for not going to the Cape. The aspects listed in the questionnaire probably do not cover the full breadth of tourist perceptions of North Cape but it is assumed that several of the most important aspects were included. As shown in Table 4.2, the most important reasons for not going to North Cape are the time limits imposed by most holiday trips, and the fact that the Cape does not fit into the tourists' itineraries. Two out of five motorists also found it too expensive to travel to the remote North Cape. The survey further shows that two-fifths of the individual foreign tourists were not especially interested in going to North Cape because they do not like places with a lot of tourists. One-third of the foreign motorists consider the Cape to be too commercialised. One in five motor tourists does not find the general North Cape area particularly interesting.

Table 4.2 The importance of reasons for not going to North Cape, for foreign motor tourists who did not visit North Cape Summer 1996, mean scores (0 to 3), and percentage finding the aspect very important and fairly important

Reason	Mean score	Percentage who find the aspect important
It takes too long to drive to North Cape	1.8	62
North Cape didn't fit into the itinerary	1.7	58
Don't like places with a lot of tourists	1.3	43
It's too expensive to travel to North Cape	1.3	41
North Cape is too commercialised	1.0	32
The area around North Cape is not particularly interesting	0.7	22
Poor accommodation in the area	0.6	17
Have been to North Cape before	0.5	15

Patterns of aspects associated with North Cape

The respondents were asked what they associate with North Cape and how important the mentioned aspects were in their perceptions of this promontory as a travel destination. Eight specific aspects associated with North Cape, as shown in Table 4.1, were included in the factor analysis. The rotated factor solution with two factors is presented in Table 4.3.

Table 4.3 Rotated factor matrix, aspects associated with North Cape, all foreign motor tourists in Norway, Summer 1996

	F1	*F2*	h^2
Unspoiled scenery	0.88	0.19	0.81
Close to nature	0.83	0.23	0.73
Monumental landscape	0.80	0.25	0.71
Midnight Sun	0.60	0.44	0.55
A romantic place	0.45	0.48	0.44
Experience a remote corner of the world	0.30	0.79	0.71
A place one should see	0.15	0.79	0.65
Europe's northernmost point	0.24	0.75	0.62
Eigenvalue	4.2	1.0	
Percentage of Variance Explained	52	13	

Experience of a monumental and unspoiled landscape (Factor 1)

Factor 1 is characterised by an understanding of North Cape as a place of unspoiled scenery, a monumental landscape and a place where one is close to nature. North Cape is also associated with the Midnight Sun. This factor further includes a view of North Cape as a romantic place. This is unconditionally the most significant of the two association structures, as it accounts for 52% of the variance in the data set.

Motorists associated with factor 1 are younger than average and they have, to a lesser extent than others, been to Norway before. German visitors are over-represented in this structure, and there is also a somewhat larger proportion than average travelling with a motor home. More than others, these motorists prefer individualistic holiday activities such as fishing and walking. To a large extent, those with a high score in factor 1 visited the fjord area of southwestern Norway, while fewer than average visited North Cape during their tour.

Experience of Europe's remote northernmost point (Factor 2)

This second factor is characterised by a perception of North Cape as a remote part of the world, an idea of North Cape as Europe's northernmost point, and an impression of the promontory as a place one should see. As is the case with factor 1, factor 2 is also correlated with a tourist comprehension of this northern headland as a romantic place and a place to watch the Midnight Sun. Some 13% of the variance in the data set is explained by factor 2.

Those with a high score in factor 2 are slightly older than average, and there is also a larger proportion of women. These motorists have visited the Cape on their holiday trip to Norway more than average in the summer of 1996. Visitors from France, Italy, Switzerland, Austria and Finland are over-represented in this structure. Motorists with a high positive score in this structure are more than averagely interested in festivals and in the urban areas of Norway, and they are also more interested in participating in organised holiday activities such as ocean fishing and rafting.

Patterns of reasons for not going to North Cape

Those foreign motorists who chose not to go to North Cape were asked why they did not visit the promontory. The tourists' answers to questions about seven specific reasons for not going to North Cape were utilised in the factor analysis. The rotated factor solution with two factors is presented in Table 4.4.

Table 4.4 Rotated factor matrix, reasons for not going to North Cape, foreign motor tourists who did not visit North Cape, Summer 1996

	F1	*F2*	h^2
North Cape is too commercialised	0.86	0.03	0.74
Don't like places with a lot of tourists	0.83	0.04	0.69
The area around North Cape is not particularly interesting	0.69	0.07	0.48
Poor accommodation in the area	0.60	0.16	0.39
It takes too long to drive to North Cape	0.03	0.88	0.77
North Cape didn't fit into the itinerary	-0.01	0.79	0.62
It's too expensive to travel to North Cape	0.25	0.69	0.54
Eigenvalue	2.6	1.7	
Percentage of Variance Explained	37	24	

The commercialised and crowded North Cape (Factor 1)

Factor 1 is correlated with an idea of North Cape as being too commercialised, a dislike of places with many tourists, and a perception of the area around North Cape as one of no particular interest. The factor is further correlated with a tourist impression of the poor quality of accommodation in the area around the headland. This association structure is called the commercialised and crowded North Cape, and accounts for 37% of the variance in the data set.

Visitors from Germany and France are over-represented in this structure, while there are fewer Swedes than average. There are no gender differences. Less than others, these motorists had decided their itinerary in advance. More than others they have visited places such as the city of Bergen and Sognefjord in southwestern Norway, and the archipelagos of Lofoten and Vesterålen and the town of Tromsø in northern Norway. Among those with a high positive score in this structure, fewer than average were of the opinion that they got their money's worth during their tour in Norway. Motorists associated with this structure are more than averagely interested in individual outdoor activities. They are also more concerned than others about environmental issues, and environmental standards have, to a large extent, been a decisive factor in their itinerary or selection of travel destinations in Norway. Fewer than average are interested in going to North Cape. Even so, half of the motorists with a high positive score in this association structure express an interest in going to North Cape, but have not yet been there.

The distant North Cape (Factor 2)

A structure called 'the distant North Cape' is correlated with an idea that it takes too long to drive to North Cape. This factor is further correlated with a view that the Cape does not fit into the tourists' itineraries, and that the foreign motor tourists find it too expensive to travel to this headland. Around 24% of the variance in the data set is explained by this factor.

Visitors from Sweden and Denmark are over-represented in this structure, and there is a larger than average proportion of women. These motorists were more likely to have decided their itinerary in advance. Motorists associated with this structure are less than averagely affected by environmental issues, and environmental standards have been a less decisive factor in their selection of travel destinations in Norway. Few of those with a high score in this factor have visited places in Northern Norway during their tour, and they are more than averagely attracted to the mountainous interior of Southern Norway. At the same time, they express a greater than average interest in going to North Cape in the future. Three in four motorists with a positive score in this structure show an interest in visiting North Cape, but have not yet been there.

Discussion

This study suggested the existence of two different general impressions of North Cape among foreign motorists in Norway. One impression is characterised by an understanding of North Cape as representing unspoiled scenery, a monumental landscape, a good place to observe the Midnight Sun and as a place where one is close to nature. The second impression is characterised by a notion of the Cape as representing a remote part of the world, an idea of North Cape as Europe's northernmost point and an impression of the famous promontory as a place one should see. Both of these general impressions of North Cape include a perception of the site as romantic but it is, to a certain extent, unclear what this romance or romanticism implies. The category of tourists associated with an impression of North Cape as a monumental and intact landscape visits this huge headland less frequently than does the average motor tourist. It seems reasonable that relatively romantic tourists (in the sense of searching for desolation and the undisturbed) are not especially attracted to a place characterised by large numbers of visitors. Since the vista of the Midnight Sun is included in this impression of the site, the experience of crowding is more or less inevitable, as the Midnight Sun by definition is visible solely around midnight – unless it is shrouded in fog from the Arctic Ocean. But some motorists may not have anticipated this concentration of tourists, even if it is well known from sources such as guidebooks (see Jacobsen *et al.*, 1998).

The understanding of North Cape as a representation of the northern edge of the European world and a place one should see frequently leads to an actual visit to the cliff. This perception seems to delineate a relatively collective gaze or, at least, an acceptance of the presence of fellow tourists, as the foreign motorists with a positive score in this structure are more than averagely interested in festivals and in the urban areas of Norway, and are also interested in participating in several organised travel activities. A proportion of these visitors appear to represent some kind of checklist tourism rather than a primary interest in the experience of nature. There is also a greater than average proportion of women with a high score in this factor. This appears to represent a departure from an earlier study of visitors at a somewhat similar promontory, Land's End in Cornwall, where female visitors were more likely to object to large numbers of visitors (Ireland, 1990: 44).

On the basis of factor analysis of reasons for not going to North Cape, this study further revealed two distinct negative impressions of the Cape among foreign motor tourists who did not visit the area during their holiday tour in Norway. One impression is labelled the commercialised and crowded North Cape. This impression is identified among those motorists who have an individualistic attitude, and who are fairly concerned about environmental issues. They consider North Cape to be too commercialised and, more than others, they also found prices in Norway to be high. Moreover, these motorists display an anti-tourist, or a relatively romantic, demeanour. One of their main reasons for not going to the Cape is that that they do not like places with many tourists.

It may seem paradoxical that one of the most remote and peripheral tourism attractions in Europe is considered to be too crowded. Several aspects contribute to this problem of image and visitor logistics. There is perforce an inevitable concentration of visitors during the short tourism season at North Cape – a season lasting only a few Arctic summer months. The northernmost part of the plateau itself is also a limited area, a situation wherein the visitors are easily visible to one another. Tourists' desire to see the Midnight Sun from the plateau contributes particularly to crowding, as this is naturally possible only around midnight, from the middle of May until the end of July. The high season at the promontory is from the beginning of July until the middle of August. In practice, most of the visitors interested in the Midnight Sun arrive there during a period of about four weeks in July, which implies that there may be more than 4000 visitors at the Cape at one time.

The Midnight Sun at the Cape is a rare experience not only because it is seen only around midnight but also because it is often overcast or foggy at the promontory during this period. A further contribution to increased crowding at the plateau is the fact that several visitors come back a second night, if they do not get a glimpse of the sun during their first night on the promontory. The impression of the site as commercialised and crowded indicates that North Cape has an image problem as a potential destination among environmentally minded and price-conscious visitors with anti-tourist or traveller attitudes. This seems further to testify to a possible change in general perceptions among the foreign visitors in this area. North Cape appears to have been relatively more important in earlier foreign tourism to Northern Norway. But this is uncertain because of the lack of historical data on foreign tourism to Norway. If the Cape really has become less important, this is possibly a result not only of image changes but also of changes in tourists' interests.

Among a proportion of the visitors in this area, there appears to be a gradual shift from a predominantly visual sightseeing tourism (often as part of a cruise), to increased interest in polysensual experiences – a manifestation of the growing use of senses other than vision in place encountering (see Jacobsen, 1994). Conceivably, easier access to the promontory and the recent increase in the volume of tourism at the Cape and in several other places in the region also make it more essential for visitors to express an anti-tourist or romantic feeling when touring Northern Scandinavia. The category of motorists associated here with an impression of North Cape as crowded and commercialised shows a notable interest in the outdoors, and they possibly also want to enjoy proximity to nature.

The other impression, based on reasons for not going to this desolate headland, is called the distant North Cape. Motorists who scored highly within this category believe that it takes too long and would be too expensive to travel to the promontory. Nor does North Cape fit into their itinerary. The impression of the Cape as distant is particularly recognised among motor tourists from Denmark and Sweden, indicating that North Cape as a symbol of the edge of Europe is perhaps not so significant, or of only minor importance, to Scandinavians. Non-Scandinavians generally have longer trips to Norway, and may not mind the additional mileage to the very far North. Many of the motor tourists from the neighbouring countries also appear to be less daring in their travel dispositions and they seem to be less oriented towards 'mileage consumption' on their tours. A large proportion of these motorists are characterised by affection for the landscapes in the interior of Southern Norway. It seems that the Cape (and Northern Norway) are simply not included in the manifest travel interests or the vistas of these motorists. This further implies that the tourist notion of access is also decisive for the prospective success of a destination. But since many of them express an interest in going to North Cape in the future, it appears that they might be persuaded to go North during a later trip to Norway, especially if their impressions of barriers such as travel time, distances and expenditures are reduced.

Conclusions

This study contributes to tourism research on peripheral areas by the implementation of an empirical approach to the understanding of different impressions of an important tourism attraction on the northern outskirts of Europe. The data analysis revealed two different and distinct images of North Cape. The idea of the Cape as a monumental and unspoiled landscape where one is close to nature is mainly found among young foreign motorists with a preference for individual outdoor activities. Consequently, a kind of anti-tourist or relatively romantic demeanour appears to be an important aspect to consider for the future development of motor tourism both to the Cape and to Northern Norway in general. The category of tourists associated with an impression of North Cape as a monumental and intact landscape travels to this desolate attraction less frequently than does the average motor tourist. If one wants to entice such foreign motorists to North Cape in the future, it seems necessary to make changes both at the site and in the marketing of the attraction. Generally, there appear to be certain difficulties in attracting tourists with romantic notions to a place characterised by large numbers of visitors. But to a certain degree it still seems possible to improve the site and its promotion in the direction of relatively romantic visitors.

The notion of North Cape as a representation of the northern edge of the European world and a place one should see frequently leads to an actual visit to the cliff. Based on the method used in this paper, the main potential for bringing new motorists to the Cape is identified among those visitors associated with this sense of the promontory, as this perception represents a relatively collective tourist gaze or at least seems to imply an acceptance of the presence of quite large numbers of fellow tourists.

One limitation of this study lies with the self-reported measures of opinions and attitudes at the end of the visit to Norway. A second limitation is that the survey covers only certain aspects of the tourists' cognisance of North Cape as a destination. Despite these problems, the approach seems to be useful, and provides an insight into some interesting patterns, partly relating to theoretical concepts and heuristic typologies established in tourism research.

In conclusion, the chapter offers a simple, empirical framework of impression or image structures, relevant and meaningful both to scholars and tourism marketers. More extensive research is essential to conceive the outcome of tourist perceptions upon the development of a site such as North Cape. Future research should be aimed at a greater specification of the aspects associated with the destination, the design, architecture, layout and logistics of the facilities at the site.

References

Aubert, V. (1965) *The Hidden Society*. New Brunswick, NJ: Transaction Books.
Brown, J. and Lee, P. (1997) *The Rough Guide: Norway*. London: Rough Guides.

Brown, J. and Sinclair, M. (1993) *The Rough Guide: Scandinavia*. London: Rough Guides.

Clark, S. (1949) *All the Best in Scandinavia*. New York: Dodd, Mead.

Echtner, C.M. and Ritchie, J.R.B. (1991) The meaning and measurement of destination image. *Journal of Tourism Studies* 2 (2), 2–12.

Haukeland, J.V. and Rideng, A. (1997) *Utenlandsk bilturisme i Norge 1996* (Foreign Motor Tourism in Norway 1996). Report 353. Oslo: Institute of Transport Economics, Norwegian Centre for Transport Research.

Ireland, M. (1990) Come to Cornwall, come to Land's End: A study of visitor experience at a touristic sight (*Problemy Turystyki*) *Problems of Tourism* 13 (3–4), 33–53.

Jacobsen, J.K.S. (1993) Motivsegmentering av feriemarkedet i Lofoten og Vesterålen (Benefit segmentation of the tourists in Lofoten and Vesterålen). In V. Jean-Hansen and J.V. Haukeland (eds) *Reiselivsforskning i Norge* (Tourism Research in Norway). Report 194. Oslo: Institute of Transport Economics, Norwegian Centre for Transport Research.

Jacobsen, J.K.S. (1994) *Arctic Tourism and Global Tourism Trends*. Research Report No. 37. Thunder Bay, Ontario: Lakehead University Centre for Northern Studies.

Jacobsen, J.K.S. (1997a) The making of an attraction: The case of North Cape. *Annals of Tourism Research* 24 (2), 341–56.

Jacobsen, J.K.S. (1997b) *Utenlandsk bilturisme i Nord-Norge* (Foreign Motor Tourism in Northern Norway). Report 354. Oslo: Institute of Transport Economics, Norwegian Centre for Transport Research.

Jacobsen, J.K.S., Heimtun, B. and Nordbakke, S.T.D. (1998) *Det nordlige Norges image. Innholdsanalyse av utenlandske reisehåndbøker* (The Image of Northern Norway. Content Analysis of Foreign Travel Guidebooks). Report 398. Oslo: Institute of Transport Economics, Norwegian Centre for Transport Research.

Kim, J.-O. and Mueller, C.W. (1978) *Factor Analysis. Statistical Methods and Practical Issues*. Sage University Paper Series on Quantitative Applications in the Social Sciences, Series No. 07-014. Beverly Hills , CA: Sage.

Krippendorf, J. (1987) Ecological approach to tourism marketing. *Tourism Management* 8 (2), 174–6.

Krogh, L., Prebensen, N., Midtgard, M.R., Sletvold, O., and Viken, A. (1996) *Nordkapp – fra hjørnestein til byggestein i Finnmarks reiseliv* (North Cape – from cornerstone to building brick in Finnmark's tourism). Alta: Finnmark Research Centre.

Leiper, N. (1990) Tourist attraction systems. *Annals of Tourism Research* 17, 367–84.

Malhotra, N.K. (1993) *Marketing Research. An Applied Orientation*. Englewood Cliffs, NJ: Prentice Hall.

Möbius, M. and Ster, A. (1994) *Lappland. Richtig Reisen*. Cologne: DuMont.

Pearce, P.L. (1982) *The Social Psychology of Tourist Behaviour*. Sydney: Pergamon Press.

Ryall, A. and Veiteberg, J. (1991) *En kvinnelig oppdagelsesreisende i det unge Norge* (A female explorer in young Norway). Oslo: Pax.

Smith, V.L. (1977) Introduction. In V.L. Smith (ed.) *Hosts and Guests: The Anthropology of Tourism*. Philadelphia, PA: University of Pennsylvania Press.

Taylor-Wilkie, D. (ed.) (1994) *Norway*. Insight Guides. Singapore: Apa.

Taylor-Wilkie, D. (1996) *Discover Scandinavia*. Oxford: Berlitz.

Thirud, Å.P. (1994) Landscapes in tourism advertising: A study on narrative geography in popular media. Masters thesis, University of Oslo, School of Cultural and Social Studies, Oslo.

Tonboe, J. (1994) From culture to nature – and from holiday to everyday. Paper presented at the XIIIth World Congress of Sociology, Bielefeld, 18–23 July.

Towner, J. (1985) The Grand Tour: A key phase in the history of tourism. *Annals of Tourism Research* 12, 297–333.

Urry, J. (1990) *The Tourist Gaze*. London: Sage.

Viken, A. (1989) *The North Cape Skyline, Nordkapp sett med turistøyne* (North Cape in the eyes of the tourists). Alta: Finnmark College.

Ward, S.V. and Gold, J.R. (1994) Introduction. In J. R. Gold and S.V. Ward (eds) *Place Promotion*. Chichester: John Wiley.

Chapter 5

Farm Accommodation and Agricultural Heritage in Orkney

JOY GLADSTONE AND ANGELA MORRIS

Rural areas have long played an important role in leisure and tourism throughout the world. However, in recent years, as many people have become more environmentally conscious, so tourism to a more remote and a more romantically viewed rural environment has become increasingly popular.

This chapter reports on selected findings on farm accommodation and attractions in Orkney undertaken by the authors as part of a research project for the Scottish Office Agriculture, Environment and Fisheries Department (SOAEFD). The study was undertaken during 1996 and 1997 using structured interviews with staff from each of the Area Tourist Boards in Scotland, face-to-face interviews with a sample of farm accommodation providers in three contrasting areas of Scotland, with postal questionnaires sent to the remainder of the farm accommodation providers in these areas as well as to agricultural heritage attractions.

Farm tourism has been narrowed in this study to reflect accommodation-related activities on farms. This may involve the letting of serviced rooms, e.g. Bed & Breakfast (B&B), self-catering accommodation, camping/caravans, bunk-houses or cottages. Other areas of this research study addressed issues concerning agricultural heritage and some of these pertaining to Orkney will be raised.

Background to Orkney

Orkney is made up of a group of more than 70 islands, holms and skerries lying 15 km off the northernmost tip of Scotland (Burgher, 1991). Orkney is nearer to Oslo (805 km) than it is to London (933 km) and was under the rule of the Kings of Norway until 1468. The population of Orkney in 1995 was 19,760 persons on an overall land area of 99,165 hectares (Scottish Office, 1995), giving a population density of 0.2 people per hectare. The farms were predominantly cattle and sheep rearing, with some cereal production, 81.9% of the land being in agricultural production.

Since the first settlers arrived in the Orkney Archipelago 5000 years ago, farming and fishing have been the mainstay of the communities in this remote and decidedly peripheral area. During the two world wars, Orkney farms made substantial profits through providing supplies for the Royal Navy base at Scapa Flow, culminating in provisioning a garrison force of 60,000 people in the early days of the Second World War. Such profits enabled the Orkney farmers to buy their farms from the estate owners. More recently, the completion of the abattoir at Kirkwall in the 1970s meant that finished meat could be exported to the mainland and further afield, rather than the transport of live animals for export on the hoof. In the 1990s, the BSE ('mad cow') crisis, coupled with changing consumer demands for meat and the increase in vegetarianism, added to the earlier European Union beef mountains, resulted in a serious loss of confidence in the farming sector and increased levels of farm indebtedness to the banks. This, in turn, has renewed interest in the diversification of farm businesses.

Access to Orkney

The main approach is by sea from Scrabster on the mainland of Scotland to Stromness on the mainland of Orkney, across the turbulent waters of the Pentland Firth, a narrow channel through which the tides of the Atlantic Ocean and the North Sea pour back and forth twice daily. The P&O Scottish Ferries vessel, the MV St Ola, capacity for 500 passengers and 120 cars, operates its one and three-quarter hour crossing every day throughout the year, weather permitting, with increased numbers of sailings during the summer months. For foot passengers, from 1 May to 30 September, the John O'Groats ferry, the MV Pentland Venture takes just 45 minutes to transport up to 250 passengers and bicycles from John O'Groats in Scotland to Burwick on Orkney, where passengers are met by buses for onward transfer northwards, over the Churchill Barriers, which connect the southern islands of South Ronaldsay and Burray to the Orkney mainland, and thence to the Islands' capital, Kirkwall. A third sea travel option is available, linking Aberdeen, Shetland and Orkney, where 400 passengers and 200 cars can be accommodated on the MV St Sunniva, a roll-on/roll-off vessel, fitted with stabilisers, whose crossing from Aberdeen to Stromness takes between eight and ten hours. Alternatively, visitors can fly to Kirkwall from Aberdeen, Glasgow, Edinburgh and Inverness, with connections from London Heathrow, Birmingham and Manchester. Flights, however, are expensive, but often fully booked in the peak, i.e. summer, season.

> The air is temperately cold, and the night so clear that in the middle of June one may see to read all night long; and the days in winter are by consequence very short. Their winters here are commonly more subject to rain than snow, for the sea air dissolves the latter. The winds are often very boisterous in this country. (Martin Martin, circa 1695)

Farm Tourism

Tourism is considered to be extremely important to the process of social and economic regeneration (Sharpley & Sharpley, 1997). Rural tourism enterprises do not differ significantly from tourism enterprises in general, in that the consumer requires accommodation, catering and entertainment facilities. However, the exception to this is farm tourism where the tourist activity is closely intertwined with farm activities and often with the viability of the household economy. The agriculturalists treat farm tourism as a category of farm diversification, while the tourism researchers view it as a sector of rural tourism (Clarke, 1996).

The demand for farm tourism can be viewed as having been fuelled by three factors:

(1) growth in the short breaks holiday market;
(2) growth in the demand for activity-based holidays; and
(3) growth in numbers of consumers reacting against mass tourism.

In addition to this, the urbanisation of the population which has taken place over the last four or five decades, gives rise to the need to (re)experience one's childhood or the lives of not so very distant ancestors (Hjalager, 1996).

As Neil Davidson (1998) describes in *The Scotsman*, when reporting on staying on a farm in South Ronaldsay, Orkney:

> Now, along with a variety of enterprises, they [Mike Roberts and Christina Sargent] offer WOOFing holidays [Working On Organic Farms] for stressed urbanites prepared to trade some hard graft for bunkhouse accommodation, plenty of fresh air and some superb smelling food.

Because of agricultural over-production in both Europe and North America, farm diversification has been viewed as a method of survival for some farm businesses, with tourism thought to be one of the more attractive and economically viable options open to farmers. In the UK, the Farm Diversification Grant Scheme was introduced in 1988, giving grants of 25% on capital investment projects and 50% on marketing costs, up to a stated maximum amount. In 1991 the capital grants on farm accommodation were withdrawn and in early 1993 this entire grant scheme was closed. The reason given by the Treasury for this cut in public expenditure was that diversification was then a well-established feature of farm businesses. Now, in the 21st century, as the profitability of agriculture has declined, there is renewed interest in diversification, as an almost desperate measure to keep the farm together. Farm tourism has changed from being a provider of pin-money, to actually keeping the farm viable in some cases (Clarke, 1996).

Considerable information, reports and survey results exist on farm tourism in other parts of the UK (Bouquet & Winter, 1987; Denman &

Denman, 1993, 1994), but it was noted by the researchers at SAC that the significance of farm tourism in Scotland had been largely overlooked, particularly from the point of view of providing much needed regeneration in rural Scotland. It was felt important that not only should the Tourist Boards provide their views, but that the proprietors themselves should be surveyed for their insights. Hence this piece of research was commissioned by the SOAEFD, and undertaken by the authors at SAC.

Study Methodology

The initial contextual work for this project involved visits to each of the Tourist Board areas to look at the extent and diversity of farm tourism accommodation and agricultural heritage attractions. A literature review was undertaken which enabled the authors to be selective in arranging representative visits and to be critical in the approach taken to question-naire design.

The visits provided an overview of the scale and diversity of farm tourism and agricultural heritage attractions generally in Scotland. As a result of the visits it was decided to complement the general overview with more detailed study of three areas: the Orkney Archipelago, Perthshire and South Ayrshire, representing examples from north, central and southern Scotland respectively. This chapter concentrates on Orkney as the most geographically peripheral of the three areas.

Inventories of farm-based tourist accommodation and agricultural heri-tage attractions were compiled. The Area Tourist Board (ATB) accommo-dation guide for Orkney was used to compile inventories of farm-tourism accommodation. This was easily done because farm B&Bs and self-catering cottages attached to farms all display a tractor symbol. The inventory of agricultural heritage attractions was compiled from the 1996 *Scotland Groups Guide* (STB, 1996).

The main concerns in this study were the attitudes and experiences of those involved with the provision of farm tourism and agricultural heritage attractions. It was also interesting to examine how farm tourism and agri-cultural heritage are regarded by the ATBs and how they feature in their tourism policies. To this end representatives from each of the 14 ATBs throughout Scotland were contacted to arrange structured interviews.

Interviews were conducted with representatives of 11 of the ATBs, which proved to be both interesting and useful. The Chief Executive of the Orkney Tourist Board (Taylor, 1996) emphasised the importance of agricul-ture to the Orkney tourist industry, stating that farming characterises Orkney as it is a living, working, agricultural landscape where visitors comment about the cattle and the greenness. Orkney food, particularly home-produced beef, lamb, oats and shellfish, has become very popular. There is a rich agricultural heritage, ranging from the seaweed-eating

North Ronaldsay breed of sheep, to the Orkney Agricultural Show, held annually in August, to which many Orcadians in exile return each year. A working group of organisations is evaluating the links between the landscape of the past and that of the present, preparing a bid for World Heritage Status. However, it is felt that the incomers [*ferry loupers*] are more interested in developing farm tourism than are the locals, which can tend to dampen the authenticity of the visitor experience and may erode traditional ways of life. There was perceived to be a danger that Orkney might become a theme park, with farmers acting out a part.

For the survey in Orkney, the names and addresses of 12 farm-accommodation providers were obtained by means of a random sample. Each proprietor was contacted, in the first instance, by letter. This was then followed up by a telephone call to arrange an interview. Respondents were interviewed face-to-face, using a semi-structured questionnaire. A postal questionnaire was sent to the remaining accommodation providers in each of the three study areas.

Overall Findings: Orkney, Perthshire and South Ayrshire

In total, 88 questionnaires were completed, 33 (38%) by face-to-face interviews and 55 (52%) by post. Eighty of the 88 respondents (91%) were female and 54 (61%) had been brought up on a farm. At the time of the survey, 27 (31%) had employment off the farm, but the majority did not. Concerning farm work, 10 (11%) worked on the farm full-time, 25 (28%) part-time, 24 (27%) occasionally, but 29 (33%) never worked on the farm. On average, their families were made up of 2.6 children; in total the respondents had 228 children, of whom 127 were males (56%) and 101 females (44%).

The survey revealed that 18 businesses (20%) had been established before 1980. Closer examination of the data shows that the majority of the tourism enterprises were set up after 1988, possibly reflecting the grants available for farm diversification at this time. Relatively few respondents stated that their decision to become involved in the tourism trade was related to any previous qualifications or work experience, although some had been involved in hotel management, travel operations management, catering and local council's committees in tourism. Since embarking on their tourism accommodation enterprises, 51 respondents (58%) had undertaken training courses, some of these related to tourism, such as Welcome Host and Food Hygiene Regulations.

When asked if they had consulted anyone before diversifying into tourism, 58 (67%) stated that they had not, with only 29 (33%) stating that they had sought advice. The reasons most frequently stated for starting up in farm tourism were to provide a source of income and to make use of spare accommodation. The only people involved in the operation of the tourism enterprise tended to be the respondent themselves, with part-time and occasional help from other family members, such as their offspring and spouse.

Orkney Study Area

Examination of the Orkney Tourist Board brochure for 1996 revealed that there were 14 working farm B&B providers, out of a total of 91 B&B establishments, representing 15.4% of the B&B provision in Orkney. Of the total of 90 self-catering establishments listed, 31 (34.4%) were on farms.

When evaluating the farm types, all the Orkney farms were classified as Less Favoured Areas, four being mixed farms (cattle, sheep and arable) and 10 livestock rearing farms, with one no-response. All the Orkney farms in the survey were owner-occupied. The fact that the vast majority of the farms in the overall survey were owner-occupied is not surprising, as owner-occupiers have total freedom over new uses for redundant farm cottages and other buildings.

All the 15 respondents in the Orkney sample who completed the detailed questionnaire were female with the age range 50–60 being the most well represented. All were, or had been, married. Three of the ventures had been set up in the 1970s, seven in the 1980s and the remaining five in the 1990s.

Several interesting findings emerged from this study of farm tourism in Orkney. First, the majority of respondents became involved in farm-tourism, in the first instance, because they saw it as providing an additional source of income. Most of the farm tourism businesses in the study made a profit and respondents agreed unanimously that this was a major advantage. The profits, however, were small, ranging from £500 p.a. to just over £5000 p.a., although two respondents did not know how much profit their businesses made. One of these started up her enterprise in 1977, as she had received a lot of requests from people to stay on her farm. She is now over the age of retirement, but keeps on her B&B business because she enjoys it so much, not knowing how much money, if any, she makes!

Second, while the extra income provided by farm tourism was impor-tant and an advantage, most respondents emphasised that this was not the only reason for doing it. Nearly all respondents emphasised that providing farm-based tourist accommodation allowed them to meet interesting people and that they valued this aspect of the job highly.

Third, farm tourism is very much a family business. While the day-to-day responsibility for running the business rests with the wife, other family members help out on a part-time or occasional basis. In return, in addition to providing the tourism accommodation, 11 respon-dents worked on the farm, varying from part-time to occasional work involving a wide variety of livestock tasks, harvesting and book-keeping. Five respondents also had employment off the farm, one even on a full-time basis.

Fourth, for the most part respondents were satisfied with the benefits that membership of Orkney Tourist Board conferred. Membership of the ATB was generally considered essential for the survival of their businesses, because of Orkney's island location, where passing trade is unknown. There were, however, some specific criticisms. These included:

(1) the requirement and additional cost of having to become a member of the Scottish Tourist Board before being allowed to become a member of Orkney Tourist Board (three respondents);
(2) the costs (two respondents);
(3) the amount of rules and regulations, e.g. the insistence on an annual inspection (one respondent);
(4) a tendency for members in the remoter parts to be forgotten (one respondent);
(5) the fact that upgrading rooms, for example by putting shelves in the corners, sometimes spoiled the character of the room (one respondent);
(6) the fact that if an establishment was up-graded then the member had to pay higher membership fees (one respondent).

Finally, family background and previous work experience are not a necessary prerequisite for entering the farm-tourism sector. Only three respondents had decided to become involved with tourism thanks to their previous work experiences, which ranged from being cooks (one in a restaurant and another in a hospital) to being a home-help. Four of the respondents had completed both the national tourist board's Welcome Host and Food Hygiene courses, while another six had completed the Welcome Host course only.

One agricultural heritage attraction in Orkney – comprising two farm museums depicting rural life in past times – completed a questionnaire which revealed that it, too, had opened to the public first in 1980, with the objective of enabling the public to benefit from local agricultural heritage. It had been established using own capital, without the aid of grants, by the current proprietor and had 10,000 visitors in 1996, a slight increase from previous years. It is open from March to October and an admission fee of £2 per adult is charged from April to September, allowing local visitors free entry in early and late season. The only other revenue comes from souvenir sales, there being neither a cafe-restaurant nor a craft shop attached. The custodian and proprietor felt that the benefits of this enterprise to local people were that it brought tourists into the area, added to the range of attractions in the area, as well as adding to the overall variety of life for the local community. For marketing purposes, the business linked with other Council Museums in Orkney and was a member of the Orkney Tourist

Board. Other marketing strategies used were to have open days and to liaise with local schools regarding curricular studies.

The two museums are described as follows in the Orkney Tourist Board Guidebook of 1998:

> *Kirbuster Farm Museum*: Glowing peats dry fish above the ancient hearth of the *firehoose* at Kirbuster Farm Museum in Birsay. Flowers flourish in the Victorian garden, and a gentle game of putting may be enjoyed on the banks of the burn.

> *Corrigall Farm Museum*: Sheep and poultry wander in and around the restored farmstead of Corrigall Farm Museum in Harray, where the circular grain kiln, weaver's loom and the horse-powered implements illustrate Orkney life a century ago.

Thus not only working farms, but also past agricultural practices have become part of the tourism product in Orkney, thereby helping to ensure that the traditional activities of a peripheral area are not entirely lost.

Conclusions

Enjoying meeting people and the capacity for hard work seem to be the most important qualifications when considering establishing a farm-tourism venture in Orkney. Most of those who responded to the survey still worked a considerable number of hours per week in the farm business, as well as sometimes having off-the-farm employment. Although some people did not seem to be involved in farm tourism for a profit motive, many indicated that their accommodation enterprise was now providing better returns than their farming enterprises. As agricultural profitability has diminished, because of the BSE crisis, low farm product prices, low confidence generally in the industry and changes to EU support measures, farm tourism has taken on a new significance to many farm businesses. Orkney is remote, but it has a uniqueness, coupled with its 'island appeal'. The pace of life there is different, the wildlife, scenery and archaeological sites world class. The Orkney Islands Council has invested much of its North Sea Oil revenue, along with EU funding, into the islands' infrastructure, by providing new piers and roll on/roll off ferry developments which link up the outlying islands to mainland Orkney, making it possible for locals and tourists to island hop within a day.

Providing farm accommodation, serviced or non-serviced, is not a new phenomenon in Orkney. Several farms diversified their businesses into the tourism sector more than three decades ago. However, it is noticeable that grant aid in the 1980s encouraged this move, along with specifically targeted schemes, such as the Agricultural Development Programme operated in the Highlands and Islands of Scotland. Agricultural recessionary periods, such as those being experienced in the late 1990s, where farm incomes have collapsed, thanks to poor demand for finished products nationally and internationally, mean that peripheral areas can be much more severely affected than those on the mainland. The challenge facing the rural community in Orkney is how to survive by finding new products, agricultural and non-agricultural, and new export markets. Already food processing, as well as adding value to local produce, with a strong marketing image of *Made in Orkney* has been the saving of some businesses. Increased emphasis is being placed on the rural traditions of high-quality food, from herrings to premium beef, high-quality Orkney beer, brewed from bere, the ancient form of barley grown in the islands, whisky from the Highland Park distillery and oatmeal for bannocks and oatcakes. Food tourism trails, along with the concept of food festivals, have another dimension to add to the existing Orkney festivals and traditions (St Magnus Music Festival in June, the Science Festival in September and the Traditional Folk Music Festival in May), for tourists, exiled Orcadians and locals alike.

Already renowned for its wildlife interest holidays, which are packaged by private operators – along with archaeological site visits – into island discovery tours, Orkney, though sparsely populated, has found its identity and presented this to the rest of Europe, if not further afield. In order truly to claim to have rural tourism founded on sustainable principles, the management plan for the proposed World Heritage Site must identify the pressures increasing visitor numbers will place on the very remote and peripheral area which the tourists come to experience, and seek solutions to these problems.

Having its own Area Tourist Board, with very strong connections and influence, with a Chief Executive who is committed to rural tourism and agricultural heritage attractions development, gives Orkney the edge over many other regions, islands and areas of Scotland. This is a strength which it must continue to use. As several of the respondents pointed out, Orkney has no passing tourist trade, so membership of and commitment to the Orkney Tourist Board is essential to their survival and future.

In the words of one of the farm accommodation respondents:

> Orkney is an expensive place to get to, so people want something good when they get here. Provide a warm welcome. Be prepared to let visitors explore the farm. Go for it!

Acknowledgements

The research upon which this chapter is based has been part-funded by the Scottish Office Agriculture, Environment and Fisheries Department and is part of a longer-term project undertaken by the Scottish Agricultural College.

References

Bouquet, M. and Winter, M. (1987) *Who from Their Labours Rest? Conflict and Practice in Rural Tourism*. Aldershot: Avebury.

Burgher, L. (1991) *Orkney: An Illustrated Architectural Guide*. Edinburgh: RIAS.

Clarke, J. (1996) Farm Tourism. *Insights*. BTA/ETB, January, pp. 19–25.

Davidson, N. (1998) Stones, bones and shopping. *The Scotsman* (19 September, pp. 18–20).

Denman, R. (1994) Green tourism and farming. In J.M. Fladmark (ed.) *Cultural Tourism*. Oxford: Donhead.

Denman, R. and Denman, J. (1993) The Farm Tourism Market, research report for the English Tourist Board and other partners.

Hjalager, A. (1996) Agricultural diversification into tourism: Evidence of a European Community development programme. *Tourism Management* 17, 103–11.

Martin, M. (1994) *A Description of the Western Isles of Scotland* (p. 350). Edinburgh: Birlinn (first published c. 1695).

Orkney Tourist Board (1998) Spring, Summer, Winter brochures.

Scottish Office (1995) *The New Councils*. Statistical Report. Scotland: HMSO.

Scottish Tourist Board (1996) *Scotland Groups Guide*. Edinburgh: STB.

Sharpley, R. and Sharpley, M. (1997) *Rural Tourism: An Introduction*. London: International Thomson Business Press.

Taylor, C. (1996) Chief Executive, Orkney Tourist Board, personal communication, 7 August.

Chapter 6

The Fall and Rise of Peripherality: Tourism and Restructuring on Bute

STEVEN BOYNE, DEREK HALL AND CLAIRE GALLAGHER

The argument of this chapter is that the changing nature of the UK tourism market has rendered the Western Scottish island of Bute more peripheral during the course of the 20th century. This process has two dimensions. Until the Second World War, Bute was a central element in the mass leisure product of the Clyde Estuary, whereby the large urban markets of Glasgow and the Scottish central belt would take to the many Clyde steamers to go 'doon the watter' – to the mainland seaside locations and island resorts – for their summer holidays – especially during the Glasgow Fair weeks – and bank holiday excursions. This pattern of leisure never recovered from the disruptions of the Second World War, and particularly from the later 1950s Bute lost its mass market appeal as Mediterranean and longer-haul packages began to supersede UK coastal resorts. Unlike many UK resorts, however, Bute also lost much of the transport infrastructure which had connected it to its markets, as the concept of cruising the Clyde and the vessels which facilitated it largely disappeared, to leave a remnant series of point-to-point ferry services and one lone summer excursion paddle steamer.

Latterly, as part of a programme of economic regeneration, attempts to restructure the island's tourism product in terms of niche segmentation have tried to focus on particular distinctive characteristics and resources of the island – heritage, land environment, water – whereby, emphasising the uniqueness of place, notions of peripherality and exoticism have been enhanced, especially for English and overseas markets.

Within this context, the chapter draws upon research undertaken at the Scottish Agricultural College as part of a wider Scottish Office supported research programme on the impacts of tourism in rural Scotland. In relation to Bute, it involved a face-to-face personal interview questionnaire survey which was administered during the summer of 1997 to a structured sample of 30 residents, members of social organisations and employees of the tourism industry on the island. The questionnaire comprised a total of 61 questions – both structured and open-ended – on perceptions of tourism development and employment and their relationships with other aspects of local social and economic development.

As an organising framework, it is argued in this chapter that Bute has become more peripheral (1) in terms of accessibility as a result of the rationalisation of Clyde estuary transport following mass market desertion; (2) in relation to market restructuring, moving from a position of centrality in relation to urban Scottish markets to one of marginality in relation to English, European and North American markets; and (3) by virtue of its product re-orientation from mass coastal to niche segmented uniqueness and relative exoticism.

There have come to be recognised relatively standard measures of peripherality. Objective criteria tend to cluster around economic underdevelopment and geographical peripherality to main centres of economic activity, low economic growth, dependence on primary economic activity with limited employment opportunities, low per capita income levels, distance and accessibility, emigration, limited education opportunities, distortion of social structures, lower population densities than core regions (Grimes, 1992; Wanhill, 1997), and a lack of political influence (Hills & Lundgren, 1977; Weaver, 1988). These geographic, economic, demographic and political criteria are called the concrete-practical perspective elements by Blomgren and Sørensen (1998).

Of course, peripherality need not be viewed negatively. Distance from the centre may be an important element for tourists seeking Urry's (1990) 'extraordinary' or MacCannell's (1976) 'other', a point which is further articulated by Blomgren and Sørensen (1998: 7) and one which may perhaps be built upon by Bute's marketeers. To the tourist, these diverse perspectives on peripherality – ease of access contrasted with the search for the (distant) 'other' – may present a compromise within which balance must be sought. To the tourism marketer, however, these apparently contradictory perspectives may be harnessed to present a product which seems tailored to the short-break, niche tourism market – exoticism and adventure within easy travelling time. This tension provides a conceptually interesting variant to Ball's (1996: 35) polemic regarding peripherality's 'objective and representational domains' whereby, in this instance, the duality lies not in presenting an area's peripherality differently to *different* audiences, but in presenting it differently to the *same* audience – a point to which this chapter will return later.

Tourism is important to the Scottish economy: in 1996 12.6 million tourists spent £2.43 billion in Scotland (Scottish Tourist Board, 1997). This represents around 5% of Scottish GDP, allowing for multiplier effects, compared with 4% for the UK as a whole, but is significantly lower than for France, Spain or Ireland (British Tourist Authority, 1997; Snowdon & Thomson, 1998). Over £2 billion of the total represents *export* sales, being expenditure by visitors from outside Scotland. Estimates suggest that some 160,000 people are employed in tourism-related activities in Scotland with around 25,000 self-employed, bringing the total to 185,000 or 8% of the labour force.

Tourism will increase in importance to the Scottish economy as employment in other sectors, notably manufacturing and agriculture, continues to decline. At a local level, tourism is often the mainstay of the economy, particularly in rural areas.

Market trends present major challenges to the tourism industry in Scotland. To compete effectively with countries such as Ireland, England and France, Scottish tourism businesses must be skilled in identifying and meeting the needs of an increasingly segmented and sophisticated market, delivering a distinctive product, quality facilities and high standards of service, effectively promoted and at competitive prices. Scottish Enterprise's tourism strategy recommended adopting a market-driven approach involving strategies, projects and programmes aimed at developing new products and securing improvements to existing ones in key areas such as the accommodation sector, visitor attractions, sport and recreational facilities (Scottish Enterprise, 1992).

In Scotland the heritage industry occupies an increasingly central role in strategies for economic growth and development. This presents the frequently acknowledged paradox of building for the future on a basis reflecting on the past. Further, with political devolution and the romantic *'Hollywoodisation'* of Scottish national sentiment, there may appear an underlying political or ideological element in regions' attempting to present and promote a unique tourism image based largely on their 'heritage' (McCrone *et al.*, 1995), an element which may add extra appeal or potential repulsion, depending on the nature of the targeted market.

While economic restructuring has assisted the seeking out of new markets, it can also assist in a rejuvenation of the old (Agarwal, 1997). In both cases, convergence between tourism and economic development policies has been encouraged by partnerships between development agencies, tourism and local authorities. In the case of Scotland this involves at least local enterprise companies, area tourist boards and local district councils, although attention has been less focused on the problems and responses of existing tourist destinations, and needs to be paid more closely to the specificity of places (Meethan, 1998).

The Bute Context

The Isle of Bute – 23 km long and over 7 km wide at its broadest point – forms a long, narrow barrier between the Firth of Clyde – the wide estuary of Glasgow's great river – and the mouth of Loch Fyne, famous for its seafood. To the north it is separated from the Argyll mainland by the Kyles of Bute – a 600 m wide stretch of water designated as an Area of Outstanding National Beauty. The southern end of Bute faces south-west over to the Isle of Arran and east to the Ayrshire coast and the smaller Cumbrae islands, together with which it protects the upper reaches of the

Firth of Clyde from the excesses of frequent south-westerly gales (Weyndling, 1996: 11).

Bute has been inhabited since at least 4000 BC, the earliest evidence of which is a Neolithic burial cairn and a number of burial chambers. There is also a stone circle and standing stones. Later inhabitants left their mark with a vitrified iron age fort. Rothesay, the island's capital, is an ancient town and was for many years the holiday home of the kings of Scotland. The Prince of Wales' premier Scottish title is Duke of Rothesay. It was made a royal burgh in 1401, and until local government reorganisation in 1974 was the capital of the county of Bute, which included Arran and the Cumbraes.

Bute is bisected by the Highland Boundary Fault. The North end of the island resembles much of Argyll: the rocks are metamorphic and the land is infertile moor, although much afforestation has taken place. South of the fault the rocks are old red sandstone and the land is pastoral and fertile, resembling Ayrshire. This highland–lowland dichotomy – 'Scotland in miniature' – is an underlying element of Bute's attraction, but an attribute several other islands and localities claim as their own.

There are two towns, Rothesay and Port Bannatyne, and a sizeable village, Kilchattan Bay. Most (85%) of the island's somewhat less than 7000 residents live in Rothesay, which acts as the service and administrative centre, with most of the hotels, restaurants and cafes and other indoor leisure activities. Rothesay is situated in an attractive bay, and sheltered from prevailing winds. Marketing hyperbole refers to it is as Scotland's Madeira, partly because of the warming influence of the Gulf Stream producing a lush vegetation, and partly thanks to the tortured imagination of the area's promoters. The centrepiece of Rothesay is an ancient castle which dates back to Viking times, when, in the late 11th century, there was an effort to consolidate Norse rule in the islands.

Later, the castle became a point of contention during the wars of independence against England, where it became a haven for supporters of the Scottish patriot William Wallace (*Braveheart*). The castle was laid to waste in the 17th century, and although much of it is still an impressive ruin, the Great Hall was restored to its former grandeur in 1970.

Mount Stuart, on the east side of the island between Rothesay and Kilchattan Bay, is the home of the Marquess of Bute, direct descendant of Robert the Bruce. Claimed to be Britain's finest Victorian Gothic house, its art collection, including works by Titian, Gainsborough, Brueghel and Rubens, is valued at over £115m. Following a change in family policy, the house was subject to major renovation and refurbishment and was opened to the public for the first time in 1995. Designed by Sir Robert Rowland Anderson and built in 1879, it resembles a great medieval palace 'which would not be out of place in Italy' (Sinclair, 1994: 175–6). As one of Scotland's heritage jewels, during the summer peak season Mount Stuart Estate employs around 50 people. Only islanders are employed, explicitly to help allay out-migration, and island students are taken on in the summer months to supplement the 30 all-year staff.

Bute as a Mass Attraction

Alongside other Clyde resorts, Rothesay owed its popularity as a watering hole to steamship development and its relative proximity to the industrial belt of Central Scotland. By the latter half of the 19th century a journey which had previously taken days could be made in less than two hours, and intense competition between steamship owners and railway companies reduced journey times further to just over an hour by the turn of the century. Ironically, this was considerably faster than today's journey time of an hour and a half.

In 1913, the last year of peace, steamers were making around a hundred calls per day at Rothesay, and during its halcyon years as the premier Clyde resort, the town's summer population rose to 50,000 people. Easy access to the mainland proved an attraction to the middle and upper classes, and resulted in a major expansion of the town along the two arms of the bay during the Victorian and Edwardian era. Land along the seafront was reclaimed, and an extensive promenade was completed in 1872. Large tenements were also built on the reclaimed land on the front of the town centre, but these have caused problems in recent years because of the unstable nature of their foundations. To the east an iron pier was built in 1877 to serve a growing trade. On the shoreline and in the woods behind a number of attractive villas were developed to provide holiday homes for the burgeoning middle classes. Today the pier is gone, but the buildings still stand, and are used as tea-rooms.

Indeed, until the Second World War the island was served by four piers. Rothesay pier was the main focus of steamer traffic, and boasted a handsome Scottish Baronial terminal building, which burned down in 1962. It was eventually replaced by an attractive building very similar in style to the original. Of the others, only the pier at Kilchattan Bay, to the south, reopened after the war, but lasted only until 1955.

Bute was a major naval base during the Second World War. Rothesay Bay housed a flotilla of submarines and a depot ship, while Port Bannatyne was a ship repair centre for vessels damaged in North Atlantic convoy battles. The massive Hydropathic hotel at Port Bannatyne, now demolished, acted as a base for submariners who trained for their successful attack on the German battleship *Tirpitz*. The considerable income for the island derived from these activities was lost in 1957 when relocation took the vessels and their crews to Faslane on Gare Loch. The economic impact of this removal was merely the forerunner of more significant change, as Mediterranean package tourism began to capture

Bute's visitor markets in the late 1950s and 1960s, as happened to most traditional British seaside resorts.

The island's resident population had peaked at 12,500 in 1951. As late as the mid-1950s Bute was still attracting 400,000 visitors a year. Within 20 years visitor numbers had fallen by three-quarters. Although the severe economic and social problems resulting from this were clearly recognisable, little progress was made to ameliorate them. For three decades Bute's tourism sector failed to adapt: economic decline was reflected in low levels of reinvestment in property and articulated in Rothesay's deteriorating physical fabric. Insularity exacerbated the constrained nature of economic opportunities, such that annual economic leakage to off-island retailers, especially in Greenock and Dunoon, has been estimated at £2 million (Bute Partnership Steering Group (BPSG), 1994: 4).

Although agriculture is still responsible for 85% of the island's land use, it employs just 110 people. Unemployment, at around 16% is slightly higher than the regional average. According to the 1991 census, 55.4% of Bute's 3214 households were without a car. Of the 6860 total population, 28.4% were retired and 51.3% were economically inactive. Second homes made up 6.4% of total dwellings, and (self-catering) holiday accommodation 3.0%, although a further 12.4% were registered as vacant (Argyll and Bute Council, no date). Of those in employment, 28.0% of the island's females and 18.4% of males were in distribution and catering; and 5.6% of males were in transport (GRO, 1992). Overall, Bute, and especially the burgh of Rothesay, has experienced the severest and most consistent (economic) decline anywhere in the Highlands and Islands over the last 40 years (BPSG, 1994:1).

Restructuring?

In 1994 a three-year action plan was devised, growing out of a number of reports and plans produced over the previous five years by various local and regional agencies (BPSG, 1994): Highlands and Islands Enterprise (HIE) overall strategy, Argyll and the Islands Enterprise (AIE) business plan, Argyll and Bute District Council (ABDC) local plan, Strathclyde Region's structure plan and economic strategy. The strategy behind the action plan was to reverse the long-term decline of the Bute economy and to improve its competitive position in relation to other areas. A number of short-term projects were put forward for implementation over a three- to five-year period (Table 6.1). The tourism component of the strategy aimed to develop Bute as a quality destination, emphasising heritage and environmental sustainability. A working party *Beyond Bute 2000*, was established to sustain the island's economic regeneration. It comprises representatives from ABDC, AIE and the Area Tourist Board (ATB).

In its SWOT (Strengths, Weaknesses, Opportunities, Threats) analysis, the development strategy suggested that Bute's tourism strengths lay in (a)

Table 6.1 Key elements of the 1994 Action Plan

- Women into Business initiative.
- Development of two flagship hotels.
- Hotel improvement programme.
- Expansion of self-catering provision.
- Development of visitor attractions through the upgrading of all-weather facilities: Winter Gardens (including a 97-seat cinema), Bute Museum, Rothesay Castle, Swimming Pool, Creamery.
- Opening of Mount Stuart to the public.
- Activity tourism development, with the need to improve the facilities, packaging and marketing of: sailing, wind-surfing, fishing (lochs stocked with rainbow and brown trout), golfing, pony-trekking (two riding schools), walking, bird-watching, archaeology (there are claimed to be 100 sites of archaeological interest, although only one is listed in the most recent national archaeological handbook (Ritchie & Ritchie, 1998); diving (numerous charted wrecks around the island).
- Upgrading of the island's three golf courses.
- A tourism management programme to emphasise environmental tourism development through a *Discover Bute* initiative.
- Development of marine tourism: yachting, transit sailing, reconstruction of Rothesay marina.
- The appointment of an events coordinator and Festival Island promotions: annual jazz and folk festival; annual international country music festival; annual Bute Highland Games, and an annual flower show.
- Upgrading tourism marketing as part of the area tourist board's Bute and Cowall promotional programme: e.g. *Scotland's Madeira* (palm trees along Rothesay's promenade).
- A community development programme.
- An appraisal of the island's ferry services.
- A programme of training and education awareness and initiatives.

Source: BPSG, 1994.

its being the nearest island to the mainland and (b) having a Victorian seafront and aspect. While the former may have been important for mass market appeal, it may now actually detract from the reconfiguring of Bute's image for niche market consumption in suggesting an all too easy accessibility. If exoticism (*Scotland's Madeira*) and adventure (*Discover Bute*) are to be promoted, proximity and ease of access may not be viewed as the most appropriate attributes to emphasise. By contrast, the Victorian atmosphere, at least that of Rothesay, could be exploited as an asset for promoting 'heritage tourism tourism' (Hjalager *et al.*, 1997), whereby the heritage of a former era of tourism activity itself can become a focus for consumption by contemporary niche heritage tourists. While it would not be appropriate to turn Rothesay into some kind of historic theme park with waitresses, hoteliers and ferry operatives dressed as if in a living stage set, the capital asset of so much Victorian heritage does merit consideration for imaginative promotion. Indeed, 'Bute remains distinctive, largely because life appears to have passed it by' (BPSG, 1994: 7), a quality with inherent niche market appeal and potential for a distinctive place-based image projection.

However, although such Victorian characteristics can be viewed as a strength, vintage architecture of this kind can present particular problems for tourism businesses and developers who are seeking to attract 'new' tourism markets, typified by highly sophisticated and demanding visitors. Cooper (1997: 132) exemplifies some of these structural limitations, describing how 'Large Victorian guest houses commonly do not have lifts, en-suite bathrooms or car parking and the rooms themselves are large and expensive to heat'. In addition, a lack of investment capital – itself a product of the decline of traditional tourism in Bute and the small-scale, owner-managed nature of the accommodation sector – exacerbates efforts to reconfigure the island's tourism product. This can be viewed as one example of how market-driven strategies for tourism restructuring or development may be impeded by the fixed nature of tourism products, particularly when these relatively static supply characteristics are contrasted with the transitory nature of contemporary tourism demand.

Low levels of investment and skills and a lack of business confidence and resources characterise the structural weaknesses identified by the island's development strategy. These are seen to be exacerbated by the recognised threats of increasing competitiveness from other islands, a spiral of decline in standards and a lack of local consensus over key development issues. The latter is seen to arise from apparent factionalism amongst the local population: a characteristic far from rare in the communities of mainland Ayrshire (see e.g., Gladstone & Hall, 1998).

With reference to Bute's geographical proximity to the mainland (point (1), p. 102), and in an attempt to develop this chapter's earlier comment on the dual nature of peripherality in relation to tourism demand, Ball, in his 1996 paper which examines local representations of peripherality, draws our attention to the fact that, at certain times and in certain contexts, it is advantageous for a locality to promote itself to different audiences as being both less and more peripheral. For example, in the image projected to potential investors or labour migrants, peripherality is played down, while for purposes of attracting development assistance from statutory bodies, notions of peripherality are accentuated. In Ball's example the task is to present different realities to different audiences; for Bute the challenge may be to present different realities to the same audience. In other words, Bute could be presented as easily accessible (important for the short-break market), while retaining the exotic imagery and sense of adventure. Such a 'doublethink' approach to tourism marketing is not entirely new to the Scottish Tourist Board (STB): the 'Scotland on your Doorstep' advertising campaign (STB: 1996: 8), which targeted travellers on budget airlines serving Scotland from London, and on the InterCity West Coast train line, promoted Scotland as easily accessible at the same time as the other, existing STB promotional campaigns continued to reinforce the exotic/wilderness/adventure imagery.

There exists a relatively limited real basis, but perhaps more importantly, a narrow perceptual basis for a restructuring programme. For example, the previously mentioned SAC survey found that, while tourism and tourism employment were viewed by a majority of interview respondents as a positive contribution to the island, a potential impediment to a restructuring programme appeared to be represented by the often narrow view taken by local people of what actually constituted tourism employment. In particular, there was a common lack of awareness of the wide range of indirectly- or part-related tourism employment forms, and the extent to which these could be retained or regenerated through tourism reconfiguration. This, in its turn, is perhaps a reflection of the relatively narrow skills and training base available for island entrepreneurs.

The persistence of tourism, however, was recognised as helping to sustain the viability of some retail and other community-based facilities which might otherwise have closed because of the limited local customer catchment and high prices. Second-home owners were viewed as helping to keep some facilities open in winter while locals travel off the island to buy in bulk at such mainland centres as Greenock.

The reconfiguring of tourism is recognised as helping to bring the community together for certain events and to assist in sustaining and enhancing local customs, such as the Bute Highland Games, International Folk and Jazz festivals. The latter, in particular, have been able to attract weekend visitors from a wide range of international markets, for whom the peripherality and relative exoticism of the island can be attractive. The degree to which these attractions represent traditional Bute values is, however, debatable.

The gender implications of post-mass tourism employment suggest that women tend to be employed in part-time capacities, as an extension of their perceived domestic role, but it was recognised that women are now more likely to be in positions of responsibility than previously, and that tourism does present one avenue, albeit relatively poorly paid, for women to achieve responsibility, either within tourism-related organisations or as self-employed entrepreneurs, and thereby enhance their social status.

Although the bases for tourism reinvigoration have been incorporated into a wider economic and urban regeneration strategy, Bute's strengths and weaknesses as an island attraction are articulated in the crucial role of transport access. Ferry services to and from the mainland are regarded as the island's lifeline, yet the nature and role of this access raise a number of problematic development issues.

First, the ferry operators, the publicly owned Caledonian MacBrayne company, receive constant criticism for their level of service, particularly in winter, when there is no service after 18.15, although traffic levels have constantly increased since 1985. Like the inhabitants in other parts of the Western Isles, the residents of Bute feel vulnerable and exposed to the vagaries both of the climate – which can prevent ferry operation for days on end in mid-winter – and of the monopolistic ferry operator's policies and time-tables. Unlike on many other islands, however, frustration for Bute residents may be exacerbated because they are situated so much closer to the mainland. Indeed, on many smaller scale maps of Scotland, the Kyles of Bute disappear completely, and Bute appears to be attached to Argyll.

The perceived inadequate level of service has an adverse impact on the local population and may exacerbate the out-migration of young people because of poor accessibility to mainland facilities. The perceived high cost of fares is widely believed to reduce tourists' spending capacity when on the island, and thus to exert a negative impact on potential tourism employment opportunities. On the other hand, relatively cheap day-trip packages organised from the mainland – through cooperation between Caledonian MacBrayne ferries, ScotRail, Stagecoach buses and Mount Stuart – while encouraging day visits and countering perceived high access costs, also reinforce the island's day-trip image and are seen to discourage overnight stays, with the result that tourism accommodation (more than 1000 beds) remains significantly under-occupied.

The question of exoticism and remoteness is only beginning to be exploited in relation to the identification of niche markets. The island does not need to depend wholly on an inadequate ferry service for tourist access, as marine-based tourism, and especially the attraction of high spending transit marine pleasure traffic, would seem an obvious target market.

The Clyde estuary is ideally placed to exploit a continuing growth in boat ownership: marinas have been developing along the mainland coast since the 1970s. As part of the 1994 strategy the outer harbour in Rothesay has been redeveloped with floating pontoons to service boat owners, and this has already attracted a new type of more affluent tourist to the island. Yet high-quality facilities and attractions are required in order to encourage them to extend their stay (even if accommodation is onboard) and to generate increased spending.

Of Baum's (1997: 33) 'island tourism fascination factors', Bute possesses the intrinsic qualities of 'small, discrete size, across the sea but not too far and different but familiar'. The island's post-mass tourism era can certainly be characterised as 'slower pace, back a bit in time', although attempts at reconfiguration are emphasising 'distinctive niche attractions', including a 'water-focused society' with activity tourism pursuits which can exploit a limited 'wilderness environment'.

Although peripherality tends to be associated with a lack of political power, in 1996 the reorganised Argyll and Bute district council chose Rothesay to site its European and business development division. A business park has been established in Rothesay, and, as a highly publicised incentive for incomers, housing is claimed to be around 30% cheaper than on the mainland (Mackenzie, 1997). In addition, not least because of an influx of European funds, the island currently enjoys a growing manufacturing sector, most notably the production of cheese, circuit boards and fabrics. European regional aid such as this, designed to improve economic and social cohesion between peripheral and central areas of the European Union, and aimed at business in general, is identified by Wanhill (1997) as having greater importance for the tourism sector than specific tourism-related policies.

Bute is promoted on a number of websites. Since late 1998 a dedicated site has been produced by local small businesses (Isle-of-Bute-com, 1998), supported by Argyll and the Islands Enterprise whose own website, promoting, for example, opportunities for voluntary organisations in LEADER II projects (Argyll and the Islands Enterprise, 1999), is aimed at providing information for the islands as well as promoting them. Promotional strategies such as this, utilising new technologies, may help the small- and medium- and particularly micro-tourism businesses which characterise many peripheral destinations overcome the financial barriers which prohibit them from marketing their product directly to specific target markets.

Conclusions

The Bute situation replicates a number of the characteristics identified by Meethan (1998) in relation to the 'old tourism' resorts of south-west England. Market fragmentation and specialisation have resulted in competition with post-industrial areas for the domestic market, competition for the domestic market with outbound overseas destinations, and competition for the international market of inbound overseas tourists. The organisational structures of local administration, economic development and tourism promotion agencies have changed during Bute's re-imaging, and tensions exist within and between them. The development of public-private partnerships and the belated emergence of a subregional economic regeneration policy which incorporates tourism have been complemented and often buttressed by the availability of European Union (EU) funding.

In so doing, the move towards 'new tourism' has both consciously and unconsciously reinforced the island's peripherality in terms of the markets being targeted and image being promoted. Paradoxically, such reconfiguring is taking place within the framework of economic development policies which seek to reinforce Bute's mainland, UK and European linkages and roles, for some of which at least, peripherality is not conducive to encouraging employment generation.

Further, there has been no universal shift from one mode of tourism to another: in the Bute case what is being experienced is a coexistence of both mass and niche specialist modes within a particular spatial context. In an age of globalisation and transition to new forms of tourism and development strategies on the back of economic restructuring, localities and their specific milieux are taking on a new role in redefining themselves. Bute continues to struggle with such a role.

Acknowledgements

The research upon which this paper is based has been part-funded by the Scottish Office Agriculture, Environment and Fisheries Department (SOAEFD), and is part of a longer-term project undertaken by the Scottish Agricultural College (SAC).

References

Agarwal, S. (1997) The public sector: Planning for renewal? In G. Shaw and A. Williams (eds) *The Rise and Fall of British Coastal Resorts: Cultural and Economic Perspectives* (pp. 137–58). London: Pinter.

Argyll and Bute Council (no date) *1991 Census Factsheet: Bute*. Oban: Argyll and Bute Council, Department of Planning, Development and Tourism,.

Argyll and the Islands Enterprise (1999) *Argyll and the Islands Enterprise-news* http://www.aie.co.uk/news/press/html/p_797_01.htm#2.

Ball, R. (1996) Local sensitivities and the representation of peripherality. *Journal of Transport Research* 24 (1), 27–36.

Baum, T. (1997) The fascination of islands: A tourist perspective. In D.G. Lockhart and D. Drakakis-Smith (eds) *Island Tourism: Trends and Prospects* (pp. 21–35). London: Pinter.

Blomgren, K.B. and Sørensen, A. (1998) Peripherality – factor or feature? Reflections on peripherality in tourism research. *Progress in Tourism and Hospitality Research* 4, 319–36.

British Tourist Authority (1997) *Tourism Intelligence Quarterly*. London: BTA.

Bute Partnership Steering Group (1994) *Bute Action Plan: A Development Strategy for the Isle of Bute*. Rothesay: BPSG.

Cooper, C. (1997) The environmental consequences of declining destinations. In C. Cooper and S. Wanhill (eds) *Tourism Development: Environment and Community Issues* (pp. 129–37). Chichester: Wiley.

General Register Office, Scotland (1992) *Census of Employment*. Edinburgh: GRO.

Gladstone, J. and Hall, D. (1998) Textile heritage in Scotland: Reconstructing the Irvine Valley. Paper presented at 'Innovatory approaches to culture and tourism', EUROTEX – ATLAS Conference, Rethymnon, Crete, October.

Grimes, S. (1992) Ireland: the challenge of development in the European periphery. *Geography* 77, 22–32.

Hills, T.L. and Lundgren, J. (1977) The impact of tourism in the Caribbean: A methodological study. *Annals of Tourism Research* 4, 248–266.

Hjalager, A.M., Sørensen, A., Brown F.S. and Hall, D.R. (1997) Round table discussion. Bornholm Museum of Art, Gudhjem, September.

Isle-of-Bute-com (1998) The Isle of Bute website, http://isle-of-bute.com/

MacCannell, D. (1976) *The Tourist: A New Theory of the Leisure Class*. London: Macmillan.

Mackenzie, A. (1997) Tide on the turn in Firth of Clyde. *Scotland on Sunday* (24 August).

McCrone, D., Morris, A. and Kiely, R. (1995) *Scotland – the Brand: The Making of Scottish Heritage*. Edinburgh: Edinburgh University Press.

Meethan, K. (1998) New tourism for old? Policy developments in Cornwall and Devon. *Tourism Management* 19 (6), 583–93.

Ritchie, A. and Ritchie, G. (1998) *Scotland: An Oxford Archaeological Guide*. Oxford: Oxford University Press.

Scottish Enterprise (1992) *Towards a Tourism Strategy*. Edinburgh: Scottish Enterprise.

Scottish Tourist Board (1996) *Annual Report 1995–1996*. Edinburgh: Scottish Tourist Board.

Scottish Tourist Board (1997) *Tourism in Scotland 1996*. Edinburgh: Scottish Tourist Board.

Sinclair, M. (ed.) (1994) *Scottish Island Hopping*. Edinburgh: Polygon.

Snowdon, P.J. and Thomson, K.J. (1998) Tourism in the Scottish economy. In R. MacLellan and and R. Smith (eds) *Tourism in Scotland* (pp. 70–92). London: International Thomson Business Press.

Urry, J. (1990) *The Tourist Gaze*. London: Sage.

Wanhill, S. (1997) Peripheral area tourism: A European perspective. *Progress in Tourism and Hospitality Research* 3, 47–70.

Weaver, D.B. (1988) The evolution of a 'plantation' tourism landscape on the Caribbean island of Antigua. *Tijdschrift voor Economische en Sociale Geografie* 79 (5), 319–31.

Weyndling, W. (1996) *Ferry Tales of Argyll and the Isles*. Stroud: Sutton.

Chapter 7

The Evolution of Tourism in the Tärna Mountains: Arena and Actors in a Periphery

NILS ARELL

This chapter analyses the evolution of tourism in a peripheral area with limited alternative options – the Tärna mountains of northern Sweden.

In general, areas (environments) with a diverse structure in their trade and industry sector offer a number of alternative ways and means of supporting themselves. Such areas, normally situated in the centre, or core, of a country often have a varied industrial background which over the years has undergone structural change and regeneration, and has gradually been transformed into a modern urban labour market, dominated by the production of services in all forms. It is therefore able to offer all-round competence.

It goes without saying that sparsely populated and peripheral regions have somewhat different characteristics. The municipalities in the mountainous regions of Sweden are characterised by the type of enterprises established by earlier generations of settlers and reindeer-herders. Exploitation of the large and existing natural resources could have led development in an industrial direction. The measures taken by the communities which were later put into practice to supplement an unbalanced trade and industry sector were dictated by the then prevailing norms. Thus, the industrial sector invested only in industrial solutions, often with limited yields. The public sector then became the last resort.

Many people, however, saw the tourism industry as another solution. Unusually, politicians in the municipalities all seemed to agree that, if everything else proved to be unsuccessful, one could always invest in the tourism industry. This opinion is, to some extent, still prevalent among municipal authorities in the area.

Until the 1930s, the region of Tärna had all the characteristics of a mountain community, that is to say reindeer-herding and small-scale farming, where all means of survival were taken care of. In fact all major facilities were lacking in Tärna: industrial culture, large forest enterprises, railways and accessible roads. Not surprisingly, given this lack, entrepreneurs seized the chance of developing the tourism industry when they discovered that they could make a living out of it for at least part of the year.

However, the results of development depend on how human and other resources are used at the local-to-local level and on the type of influence created by external conditions, for example the economic situation in the country, investments in competitive regions.

This chapter will explore the tension between the local and external forces in the development of tourism in the Tärna region. It is from this perspective that it is interesting to follow the development of the tourism industry, from the first steps taken during the 1920s, to the established industry of today in the area.

Aims, Issues and Sources

The aim of this chapter is to discuss the development of tourism as a viable industry in a peripheral region, that is to say, Tärna-Hemavan, situated in the mountainous region of Tärna, County of Västerbotten and how it has been dictated and shaped by different forces. The perspective of arena and actor will be emphasised, leading to the following questions and issues:

- Who are the actors?
- How have the forms and content of tourism changed the circle of players?
- How wide is the scope of action of the local micro enterprises in tourism and other commercial services when external developers and entrepreneurs have taken possession of their share of the local arena?
- What role have the municipalities played in the development of tourism in the area?
- How able is the local municipality, here Tärna, to cope with competition from other tourist resorts?

The source material used in this chapter is mainly interviews carried out during a period of some 20 years with a number of the actors involved in the region, many of whom were already engaged in the tourism industry from the 1920s onwards. I have also made use of a great deal of research and planning material collected from municipal authorities, regional authorities, lobby organisations and private companies. Finally, I have also closely followed the development of tourism in the Tärna mountains through frequent visits to the area from the 1950s onwards.

Theoretical Framework

The theoretical framework used in this paper has been defined by the concepts 'knowledge', 'competence', 'structure', 'system', 'network', 'arena' and 'actors'.

The concepts 'information', 'knowledge' and 'competence' constitute three levels of quality. Competence presupposes knowledge which, in turn, requires information. However, information cannot simply be processed without knowledge, which at the next level becomes competence. This next stage requires more than knowledge, namely the capacity to make use of and apply knowledge for a purpose. Competence is developed by constant links between the knowledge and experiences of people, tools and different elements in the physical environment (Törnqvist, 1986).

Competence can be of different categories:

- Tool-specific competence where the human–tool link is of great importance. For example, the elite downhill skier is someone with this high degree of competence.
- Sector-specific competence is first and foremost made up of information which disseminates or is linked between competences within definite sectoral limits.
- Regional-specific competence implies that the links to local and regional resources are important. This can be a question of special professional competence arising from specific local or regional natural resources.

In order to succeed locally in one's aim to start and maintain any development, competence in many areas is needed. An interesting but difficult problem to solve is the form the local (social) system should take in order to accommodate the necessary competence and contribute to a creative environment. In other words, how can you attract and hold to the competence you need? Where Tärna-Hemavan and other similar regions are concerned, these questions are of strategic importance.

In his structural theory the sociologist Anthony Giddens has a perspective of knowledge which is linked to the concept of conduct (action). According to Giddens (1979), conduct is not seen as an isolated entity with a purpose but as 'a continuous flow of conduct'. In fact, the aims and purposes of conduct are always being shaped and reshaped. The actions of people or actors are highly dependent on their knowledge or competence. Here, Giddens refers to two types of knowledge: discursive and practical. The former is that part of knowledge which can be described in words and can therefore be *discussed*. The latter – practical knowledge, which is as important – is referred to as tacit knowledge, which is coherent with the fact that it is not easy to verbalise. An aspect of conduct is that there is always an alternative to any action and that the alternatives are determined by the discursive and practical ability of the individual. No matter how able and competent the actors are, no one has a complete insight into or overall view of his/her local sphere of activity, if at all. There is, therefore, a tension between local actions and external, often unknown, conditions and means of control. This means that actions taken cannot always have the desired effects and decisions and measures may be counterproductive (Åqvist, 1992).

The compound word 'infrastructure' refers to physical installations, for example roads, streets, telecommunications (main systems) or ski lifts. However, the structure need not say anything about the functions of the installations. For example, a water-pipeline is one thing, but its function is first tested when the water is turned on. It is only then, and if everything works, that the structure becomes a system, an important quality in the system being its dynamics. As such, structure and system are (too) often used as synonyms which at times creates uncertainty.

Structures are always changing, so are systems. The structure is a requirement, often restrictive, for the system. How the system works depends on, among other things, rules and resources. The structure can even be said to represent or create conditions for stability, which can be seen as static. It is, however, easy to be caught up in a structure and experience has shown that, for example after building/investing in spatial structures, it can be very difficult to change them. Other forces, acting in the same direction and restricting our spheres of action, are linked in different ways to organisational forms and other systems of decision-making found in the private sector and also in the public administrative sector (Törnqvist, 1986).

Another aspect of the notion of systems is the geographical or spatial notion, for example interregional dependency relationships (interdependence). What is taking place in a region not only affects the local and regional conditions but it is also linked to spatial interrelationships, the flow and contact networks. This leads to open and closed systems as well as to the question of how the system should be restricted. One might ask, can one delimit a closed system? The Tärna area, until 1972 corresponding to the municipality of Tärna, could not have been seen as a closed social system in any way. It is in fact very hard to find a closed and delimited system which is not dependent on other systems.

Another word for system is network – simply described as made up of nodes and links which can be connected to other nodes, (sub)systems or networks, and carrying information of differing types. A social system, on the other hand, functions through social interactions by making use of the different types of networks.

In this study I have referred a great deal to actors and arenas. Actors can be individual people, companies of different sizes and trends, lobby organisations, public institutions and administrative areas. They appear with varying frequencies in the arena and in different constellations with differing aims. In the definition of an actor, there is the underlying concept that he/she can influence the developmental processes by his/her actions. We shall now apply these concepts to the development of tourism in Tärna.

Tourism in Tärna: An Overview

Mountain tourism in its organised form was introduced in the Tärna region in the 1920s by the Svenska Turistföreningen (STF) opening a youth hostel in Tärnaby. By the mid-1930s, farmstead-lodgings had started to be used for tourist accommodation. Full board and lodging was the most common form of accommodation during the 1950s and 1960s and it was also during the 1960s that holiday cottages came increasingly to be used. The houses which were built during the 1970s and 1980s were more like well-equipped smaller villas than cottages, and they cost more. It was by the end of the 1970s that new ownership and forms of financing such as condominiums and later, because of the effects of taxation, cooperative flats in apartment blocks were introduced. In other words, Swedish laws governing taxation had a great influence on this development.

The very high standard of the recent generation of holiday houses resulted from the fact that the older and low-standard cottages were, so to speak, removed from the rental agency market, the primary competitive factor being not the lower prices but the location and standard of the houses. For example, during the winter season, one *has* to live by the ski slope, because the average winter tourist would like to ski as much as possible in the space of one week. Time must be used effectively, logistics are of the utmost importance. After the long car or bus ride to the destination, it is as if one has to have everything within walking distance.

Improved communications have, over the years, made the Tärna mountains more accessible to tourists but, as always, it is all about comparable conditions. A number of resorts will always be further away than others. The distance from Stockholm to Tärna or from Val d'Isère will always depend on a number of other factors and considerations, not necessarily rational.

The tourism industry in the mountainous regions encompasses a range of businesses. First of all, one might think of the actual tourist enterprises: the hotels and restaurants, amusement parks and other services related to the tourism industry, for example services to skiers, hikers, anglers, cottage owners and those taking part in conferences. However, the tourism industry also involves building contractors, transport companies, investment and financial institutions and banks, as well as estate agents. All of these form part of the tourism industry to a greater or lesser degree.

If a region wants to succeed in the tourism industry, what is needed is competence in a number of areas. Developing this competence and getting tourism accepted as a serious industry takes time. When municipal and regional authorities see tourism first and foremost as a way of creating job opportunities, this need for competence may be underrated. In fact, one can find quite a number of examples. One such was the argument put forward for the building of a luxury hotel in one of the mountainous municipalities of Västerbotten, in order to create jobs to compensate for the closing-down of a mine.

The attempt to develop a tourism infrastructure in the region of Tärna and, at the same time, to keep pace with the ever growing wishes and demands of the market, as well as with competitors in other tourism areas, has been underway for over seven decades now. Taking into account integrated experiences and thanks to favourable conditions, Tärna-Hemavan has become the only mountain community in the county of Västerbotten which can compete with others in the national arena.

The community has been helped in this respect because downhill skiers from Tärnaby have excelled themselves in international competition; their domination of the sport for a number of years contributed to the tourism industry of the Tärna region. It is impossible to measure what impact Ingemar Stenmark's unique competitive talents had on the region, but it is reasonable to assume that some of the increased interest in downhill skiing could be associated with his name. Since he became famous the tourist season has centred mostly on downhill skiing, hence influencing planning, building and land use in the area. At the same time, however, the imbalance between the summer and winter seasons has deepened, a point in common with other areas in the same branch of trade.

Former generations of winter tourists in Tärna went on day-trips on skis. On the other hand, those who now visit the mountains in summer do not have very different motives from summer tourists of old.

Images of the Periods

In this section, the development and characteristics of tourism will be described during different periods of time, in order to present a picture of the way the actors and structures in the Tärna tourism industry have changed over time. The relationships between the actors will be shown graphically. However, the figures should not be seen as exact representations of the actors involved at any given epoch, but rather as an illustration of a process of development.

The periods are:

- around 1930;
- the 1950s and 1960s;
- the 1970s;
- around 1990; and
- the present.

To single out the relevant actors in the arena of Tärnaby-Hemavan is a question of definition and how this definition is made depends on one's aims. It is practically impossible to identify all the actors involved, in one way or the other, in the developmental process, let alone to have a clear

definition of them. The following are among those who have played prominent roles in this process:

- national tourism organisations, such as the Svenska Turistföreningen
  (STF) and the Skid-och Friluftsfrämjandet (SoF);
- local entrepreneurs and those closely linked with the tourist trade;
- external companies in building and construction;
- external estate agents, financial institutions and banks;
- the municipalities of Tärna (before 1972) and Storuman (after 1972)
  respectively;
- the municipally owned ski-lift company;
- regional and central authorities.

The 1930s

The first tourism in an organised form in Tärna, as in many other places
in Sweden, took place in collaboration with the Svenska Turistföreningen
(STF). The idea of establishing the STF came, however, from abroad.

The purpose of STF was to disseminate information and awareness
about our country and people, in the interest of the whole country. This was
sometimes done through having its officials travel around the country in
order to 'discover' new touristic and, at the same time, interesting natural
and cultural surroundings (milieus). During the summer of 1922, Tärnaby
was visited and it was immediately realised that the area had great potential as a tourist resort. A plot of land was bought by the STF some years later
and a youth hostel was built. From then on, the basis of tourism in Tärna
and the mountain areas of Västerbotten was established. This was in 1927,
almost 40 years after the beginning of tourism in the mountains of Jämtland
to the south and much later than the beginnings of tourism in the mountains of Norrbotten, which had started with the building of the Abisko
(1906) and Kebnekajse (1907) tourist stations.

The main reason for the late start to tourism in Västerbotten was the lack
of communications. It was only in 1924 that a railway line to the coastal
region was established and it was not until the beginning of the 1930s that a
main road was built up to Tärna; this was later extended to the Norwegian
border in 1939.

The STF was the initiator and therefore the first actor in the arena, but
very soon ideas as to how to arrange tourist trips to the mountains were
beginning to emerge. The introduction of homestead tourism (gardsturism)
attracted new groups, for example pupils and students. Local initiatives
were encouraged and the idea that tourism could bring in income took firm
roots and started to grow. During the first few years, summer tourism was
the only type of tourist activity. The tourist station opened for the first time
in winter in 1935, during the course of two Easter weeks, and thus organised winter tourism started for the first time.

What then is homestead tourism? There is some similarity between homestead tourism and the bed and breakfast lodgings found in the UK, in which one stays for a night or two at a place where such facilities are available. In Sweden, this took the form of staying at homesteads during Easter as tourists.

Homestead tourism became important during the early stages of tourism because it gave its practitioners experience, contacts and earnings, as well as contributing to the improvement of the homesteads involved. These examples further spread interest in tourism as a means of livelihood. A positive attitude and an entrepreneurial spirit were thus established.

Nevertheless the idea of homestead tourism had also originated outside. Some years back, organised trips for pupils to Sälen in the mountains of Dalarna had been arranged under the auspices of the Skid-och Friluftsfrämjandet (SoF), the other big tourism organisation in the country. Interest became so great that its activities were expanded to include the mountain regions of Västerbotten. In the Tärna area, a branch was started in Hemavan, where quite a number of people became engaged in its activities. However, just as these trips began to take on an organisational form, war came and the whole area around Tärna was closed to the public for five years. Instead of tourists, soldiers came and these were stationed in almost all the empty rooms in the homesteads throughout the war.

Figure 7.1 Tourism actors around 1930. The actors are few in number and small, and the structure is simple. The two large national organisations, STF and SoF are the only external actors

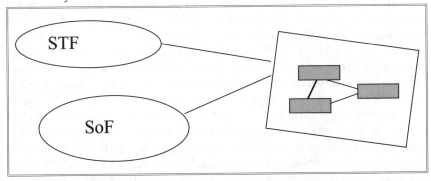

The 1950s and 1960s

After the end of the war, tourist trips started again. For a long time the bulk of the tourists were made up of soldiers who were stationed in the area during the war, and their families. For Tärna, the 1950s heralded a new epoch. The driving force in this process of modernisation was the rationalisation of the farming of mountainous areas which led to the end of the area's subsistence economies, as well as to the era of hydroelectric power stations.

The building of hydroelectric power stations started in 1952 and when it stopped 20 years later Tärna had more power stations than almost any other municipality in the country. The municipality now became one of the most important actors. This involved, first and foremost, negotiations with those building the hydroelectric power stations over how to behave in the water-rights court and in relation to the government, where they had strong support in the person of Gösta Skoglund, the then Minister of Transport and Communications. This gave the local politicians useful experience and insights into the importance of having a well-conceived strategy.

The economic gains for the municipality from the water controls were favourable on the whole. The development period took a long time, which was an advantage. Taxes rose, the municipal economy was radically improved and the number of inhabitants greatly increased as a result of immigration. The lake storage-capacity regulation provided so-called regulatory funds and other funds linked to specific conditions, while those working at the power stations increased the revenue of the municipalities through the multiplier effect.

The local labour market also changed. With the water controls, 'real' jobs became available, those needing continuity in work and specialist knowledge. Many previously unskilled workers became skilled workers. Purchasing power and consumption rose and the inhabitants of Tärna started their march towards social development.

With regard to the tourism industry, this period was of great importance because there was now the possibility of financing tourist projects and investing in the local infrastructure. Otherwise it would not have been possible to get STF and SoF interested in establishing themselves in the Tärna mountains. As for the hotels and boarding-houses built at that time, no state loans were available and, as tourism was not on an equal footing with other industries, no regional development grants were available. It was possible to get bank loans of up to half of the capital investments but the banks were not very keen on tourism projects. In this context, the municipalities stepped in and, by applying for funds linked to specific conditions and grants from the National Labour Market Board, 90% of the necessary capital was provided. Only 10% had to be raised from private funds. The funds linked to specific conditions were administered by the County Administration, and therefore applications were made whenever the need arose. Most of the funds were, however, spent on developing the infrastructure because what was good for the community was also good for the tourism industry and vice versa.

Nevertheless, the economic gains should not be used to hide the negative effects of the hydroelectric industry, for example the physical and environmental changes in the landscape, problems with fog and sand storms as well as the deterioration of fishing waters. It is ironic that the very favourable conditions laid down for the tourism industry, as a byproduct of the hydroelectric industry, were to spoil one of the most important tourist attractions, namely the water landscape.

As an actor in the arena, the Municipality of Tärna played its role to the fullest. Among the leading local politicians, it was understood that it was possible to stop the regulatory projects and therefore they had to sell themselves to the highest bidder, something they succeeded in doing.

Twenty-five years after the opening of the tourist station in Tärna, the next step was taken – the building of a mountain hotel in Hemavan, under the auspices of the SoF. The arguments for an application to finance the hotel were the same as those previously used 25 years ago:

- the desire of the state authorities to spread tourism to areas more peripheral than the mountains of Jämtland;
- the beautiful ski terrain in Tärna;
- the enormous possibilities for hiking in the mountains, mountaineering, angling as well as bathing and canoeing in the waterways of the Umeå river.

Furthermore Hemavan is on the border with Norway and economic development for the local inhabitants was emphasised, something an increased volume of tourism might bring about. If economic improvement was to take place, improved communications for the area, which follows close behind the paths of tourism' would really be needed. The hotel was opened in 1953 and the first ski lift in Västerbotten was built close to the hotel a year later.

Apart from the activities of the STF and the SoF, smaller establishments were started by individual initiatives. One local actor, Sture af Ekenstam, should be mentioned because of his exemplary entrepreneurship. More than any one else and with great energy, from the 1940s onwards Mr Ekenstam succeeded in establishing tourism as an accepted and serious industry in the municipality. He saw early on the importance of developing a wide contact network at different levels in the administrative system. This involved Tärna being made part of the tourist network both in Sweden and also more widely in the Nordic countries. Without this type of industrious local actor, no development on a wider basis can get started. Big, externally administred constructions can lead to the phenomenon of social alienation, with little support from the community. There is always the risk that smaller local actors may become dependent on a few larger actors.

By the mid-1960s, a new tourist hotel was opened in Tärnaby under the auspices of the STF. The old youth hostel needed to be supplemented by a modern all-year-round hotel. The initiative was taken by the municipality, which persuaded the STF to build and operate the hotel. The costs of the construction were covered by funds from the hydroelectric industry and other state grants. From then on, Tärna would be able to compete for tourists with Hemavan. However, it should be borne in mind that it was in Tärnaby that downhill ski racing developed as a sporting event thanks to the Fjällvinden Sporting Club, with its well-organised sports and training activities. Fjällvinden put Tärnaby on the alpine map of the world that was used to market the Tärna mountains. There is still a saying (not least in Tärna) that the tourists go to Hemavan but those wishing to do slalom-skiing stay in Tärnaby.

Figure 7.2 The 1950s and 1960s. STF and SoF have built hotels, 1 and 2. The circle of actors has been enlarged to include the Municipality of Tärna, the Regional Authorities and Vattenfall

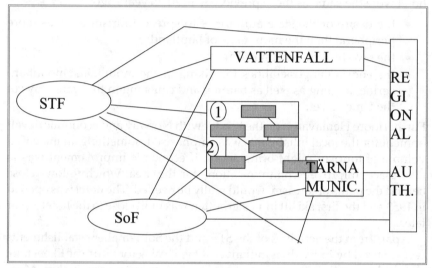

The 1970s

Several events occurred in the 1970s which affected the development of tourism. By the 1960s, people had seriously started to dream about having a cottage in the mountains and this dream was realised in the 1970s when the exploitation of the mountainous area expanded. The economic conditions for building holiday cottages were favourable and generous taxation rules meant that the whole sum of the rate of interest on loans could be deducted from one's income tax return. This, coupled with high marginal tax, meant that the net effects were great.

Parallel with this exploitation and a driving factor in its own right, downhill skiing became the big leisure activity in winter and ski-lifts were built in quick succession. The need to be near to ski slopes, ski-lifts and other social activities led to activities and facilities being concentrated in certain areas. As a consequence, land speculation began in the more attractive areas, prompting the state to step in with restrictions on land use in order to save valuable natural environments.

A large number of the cottages in Tärna were built in Hemavan and, according to a general plan for Hemavan in 1965, the settlements were to be concentrated in one area and not spread along the neighbouring valleys. There was a desire not to copy the Norwegian example, where a lot of cabins had sprouted all over the countryside instead of following a plan.

The high cost of water, drainage and other common investments was the reason for the dense concentration of the buildings. One of the stronger arguments for concentrating the building of weekend homes in one area was that it could become more densely populated, thus strengthening the profile of Hemavan as a tourist resort, with varied public entertainment and other commercial services in a small area. The association of the Jämtland mountains with the Alps was not lost because everything was linked to downhill skiing as the dominant activity. Most people wanted to live as near to the ski slopes as possible, the argument being an economic one.

The desire of the municipality to restrict and plan land use was in accordance with that of the state regarding the mountain region. This local adjustment was the cause of irritation and of angry debates about tourism and to whom it was most useful. The land-owning mountain farmers, living outside Tärnaby and Hemavan, were not allowed to sell plots of land because of restrictive land-use planing and they saw their expected gains disappear. On the other hand, land-owners in Hemavan willing to sell land for the planned leisure area were not well paid either. Those affected saw to it that the municipal local area development plan was implemented and therefore no one became rich by selling to the municipality, because it was forbidden to build on areas not included in its plans. Thus, the municipality was the winner.

A category hard hit by the concentration of tourism in Tärnaby and Hemavan were the small-scale tourist enterprises situated along the valleys by the Norwegian border. They argued that the variation in what was offered to the tourists could be greater if all expansion was not steered from the central areas. Voices were even raised against the accommodation agency of the municipal tourist office, saying that they concentrated on trying to fill the hotels in Hemavan with tourists first and the remainder was later spread all over the area. However, Sture af Ekenstam, who together with other actors at the local level was involved in the planning process, had clear opinions: 'We were aware of the importance of planning at an early stage because it is very easy to rush off at random without planning'.

An important actor in the development of tourism was and still is the Ski Lift Company, a municipally-owned company which owns the lifts and also operates a number of activities in the surrounding area. The local municipal commissioner is Chairman of the Management Committee of the company. The development of the Ski Lift Company was closely linked with the number of beds available because, according to a simple rule of thumb, a capacity of at least 500–600 beds per lift is necessary. Before constructing a new lift, one must have the number of beds needed. There-fore, any increase in the number of beds, lifts and other services must be carried out in phases.

More holiday cottages meant more beds and therefore a stronger basis for the Ski Lift Company and more possibilities for expansion. This became a key factor and now it was not the number of beds which was decisive, but how often these could be used. The fact that more and more weekend cottages were being built, but left vacant except for a couple of weeks during the season, did not result in more people buying lift cards. It then became pressing for both the municipality and the Ski Lift Company to attract as many people as possible to the weekend cottages. Therefore an effective rental agency for private cottages was set up.

Opinions differed among a number of tourism entrepreneurs about the agency. They saw it as undue competition and argued that the municipality should protect its business sector and not support the activity of the renting out of holiday cottages, because a large proportion of the market for hotels and boarding-houses would be lost in this way. However, others thought that visitor nights would decrease no matter what the Ski Lift Company decided to do, while an increase in stays at weekend cottages would benefit the retail trade, especially the food stores.

An important change affected the conditions of taxation. The right to deduct interest rates worsened and costs rose, which resulted in increased interest in renting out cottages among their owners. A fiscal technicality was introduced in the form of new ownership forms, condominiums were changed into cooperative flats and housing cooperatives were formed. But the need to rent out houses and flats remained.

At the municipal level and with regard to Tärnaby and Hemavan, the municipality of Tärna was merged with that of Stensele in 1972 to form the new municipality of Storuman, with about 9000 inhabitants, most of whom came from Stensele. This led to questions being revised about the impor-tance of tourism. Stensele is 100 km from the mountains and therefore had an entirely different view of tourism as an industry. In fact some leading local politicians saw it 'merely' as a way of satisfying people's needs for recreation and therefore basically useless. The local arena, in the form of the territorial decision-making process, had changed in other words and the part previously played by Tärna became marginalised.

The years around 1990

The end of the 1980s and the beginning of the 1990s was a period of heavy strain on public finances and an overheated building sector. Such

Figure 7.3 The 1970s. The arena has expanded with the inclusion of the Municipality of Storuman and the circle of actors is larger, Building Contractors, Credit Institutions, the Ski Lift Company, the PR-association of TärnaFjäll and a number of local tourist enterprises

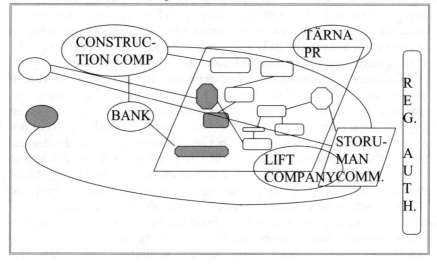

was the situation in Sweden and similar countries and so it was in the winter sport areas, which were strengthened by the hope of hosting the winter Olympics. Development was the same in Tärna-Hemavan. This period therefore became dominated by the construction boom and its consequences.

There was a great deal of activity and optimism in the Tärna area for five or six years after 1986. Many projects, some realistic, some spectacular, were launched, e.g. Tärna Fjällpark (Tärna Information Centre), an airport, an 18-hole golf course, housing projects, service areas with restaurants, a catering school and shops, as well as an expansion of the ski-lift system. Tärnaby and Hemavan were to take a couple of steps upwards in the national hierarchy.

The circle of actors changed as different projects were started. Consortia, including some of the largest construction companies in the country, were formed in order to implement large construction projects. The hotel in Hemavan, which had been sold by SoF sometime previously, was already bankrupt and had been taken over by new owners. The hotel was then expanded and modernised.

The influence on the local arena of external forces was substantial. Many were afraid that the character of Tärnaby and especially of Hemavan would be changed as a result of the unfamiliar styles of building, such as alpine chalets or Finnish-style log cabins. The construction companies frequently showed a lack of artistic sensitivity and built the same houses as in ski resorts elsewhere. Objections from the local housing committee in the municipality were few, the main objective was to keep a high profile as far as building activities were concerned. What is not being built here is being built somewhere else and then the competition will increase!

Estimates by bankers and estate agents were presented to potential buyers of these lavish holiday cottages and cooperative flats which bordered on the fraudulent. Such estimates included unrealistic promises of favourable tax breaks and, according to a local expert who cannot be named, unrealistic suggestions of potential profits. According to careful calculations, owners would be able to rent out their flats, etc. for at least 10 weeks in the winter months, at high prices, which covered almost the whole season, as well as for a further five weeks. Another false impression given was that the season was gradually becoming longer. If the buyer therefore was prepared not to use his/her house or cooperative flat during the season, the investments made would cover the expenses of the house! Many accepted these arguments without question but, after facing brutal economic realities, later added to the negative picture of mountain tourism.

When bankruptcy became known within the hotel and restaurant industry, warning voices were raised because the whole of the mountain tourism industry and its cooperative partners in the area were threatened, unless long-term planning, continuity and stability were created. The threatening picture was clear enough. The volume of investments was larger and more cost demanding than before and therefore the economic risks were greater. The demand for customers increased, as well as the need for effective marketing in a market which was not growing.

The resources for such strategic investments were limited and this fact forced the tourism companies and the public relations associations to reorganise and to intensify their marketing. Solidarity at the local level was thereby put on trial. There was capital to carry on with large construction projects but not to market them in the Stockholm area or other markets. The investments made greatly increased what was available to tourists: lift systems were expanded, hotel and restaurant capacities increased. Holiday cottages now formed the basis of the tourist trade and the hotels were marginal in relation to bed capacity. What was lacking were tourists in large numbers. Tourists seemed to form a sort of spot market.

A category of tourists who had been around for a long time but who now became economically important were those on snowmobiles. They showed other interests and consumption trends than the traditional tourists on skis. They had, first and foremost, different movement patterns, which resulted in the municipalities placing restrictions on driving snowmobiles in the populated areas. This proved favourable towards those renting out cottages and other installations outside Tärnaby and Hemavan.

The structure of the actors is now difficult to grasp. Some of them are marked in Figure 7.4. There are numerous external actors which involve new ownership constellations. Many of the established hotel and

Figure 7.4 Around the 1990s

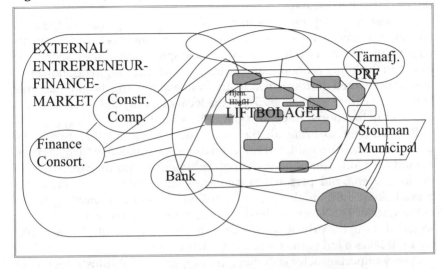

boarding-house establishments have changed owners or have become part of new combinations. New actors have established themselves through some of the construction projects implemented. Some have also ceased to exist. The complexity has increased and it is difficult to get an overview of the network.

The Situation Today

The economic climate has changed during the past five years. Building construction works have stopped. The real-estate market in Tärnaby-Hemavan is seen by estate agents as virtually dead; prices have fallen to less than half those of the 1990s. Attention is now focused more towards the general economy than towards tourism. Many have seen the value of their holiday houses and cooperative flats tumble. The regional market, which is the issue here, and which is no greater than all the potential interested parties of a weekend cottage in the mountains, is aware of the structure and risks of the market.

At the same time, many actors, local as well as external, have realised that it is time to speculate in low-value tourist installations and estates. Therefore, new combinations of owners are always being formed, with different motives for their actions. There has been a blend of knowledgeable people in this line of trade, manipulating financial companies and national construction companies as well as different categories of individuals. With each new group of actors, local influence over the process of development tends to decrease. There is a risk that the continuity of many of the earlier activities characteristic of the area will be lost. There is also a fear that people have invested in and established a structure from which it can be difficult to escape.

My description of the 1990s may evoke a negative picture of the area. However, many of the problems resulted from misguided investments which had their basis in the over-optimistic spirit of the times, soon to be frozen in the biting economic and political winds blowing. This, however, has not prevented the tourism industry from maintaining its dominant role in the Tärna area, with some 75% of the local economy in Hemavan and a turnover in the tourist trade of about SEK 145 million.

It is difficult to bring all the local associations together under the umbrella of the Tärnafjällens Public Relations Association, which has been around for a long time, and to define a common aim for their activities. In the local arena, old personal antagonisms and conflicts of interest still prevail. Some individuals in central positions are seen as stumbling blocks in the system. This is where the difference between the private and public sectors lies – in the private sector, actors come and go, while, in the public sector, it takes a long time for actors to change.

A very important actor is the Ski Lift Company. Its role illustrates part of the problem of the shifting border between private and public economies. Basically, no individual can foot the bill for the large investments needed to install lifts or for costly machine parts for maintenance and preparation of pistes. This is an undertaking for the public sector. The municipality and county council have used different sources of financing, e.g. funds to be used for specific conditions and other state grants, as we have seen previously. Over the past few years, the Ski Lift Company has had an effect on private companies, since it has started competing in areas where private tourist enterprises have had their niches, such as ski schools, the renting and selling of skiing outfits and accommodation agencies, etc. With the help of the municipality, the Ski Lift Company can exert pressure and influence conditions, even when the official line of the municipality is not to engage in the trade and industry sector. But basically the Ski Lift Company could very well be a municipal administrative organ. It should, however, be mentioned here that previously the municipality was much more involved in the sector, for example, by being joint owner of the Hemavan Mountain Hotel as well as of the Tärnaby Tourist Hotel, and by engaging in a number of other activities which could have been part of the private sector.

In June 1997 a development conference was held in Hemavan. The organiser was the Public Relations Association of Tärnafjällen (TPR) which wanted to act as a unifying force for local entrepreneurs and other interested partners in the continued development of the tourism industry. The aim was to create awareness of the necessity to work, if not towards the same goal, at least in the same direction. Another aim was to uncover closed structures which threatened to strangle creativity. The role of TPR was central and will remain so in future. A relationship of special importance is that with the municipality.

The present situation can be expressed in different ways. The tourist who does not own any property in the area need not worry about what lies behind. The sales figures for lift cards, reservations and the turnover in tourist-related activities have been good during the past few years, especially in relation to other ski resorts.

Marketing is focused more towards younger people, with the introduction of new methods of downhill skiing and more entertainment in the evenings. This development is, however, not without its problems because the alternatives for age groups with other demands on evening entertainment are limited. A marked disco profile would probably deter a large part of the middle-aged group, which has great purchasing power. The local profile no longer has any real value, rather it is a matter of copying successful formulas from other places.

Conclusions

In conclusion, the following observations regarding the rise of tourism in Tärnaby-Hemavan should be made.

From the perspective of the STF, the community of Tärna was virgin territory at the beginning of the 1920s. The establishment of the first tourism installations gave the local inhabitants the possibility of making a living from tourism. During the 1930s, know-how on what local forms such installations could take developed. Everything was on a small scale. The knowledge which developed over many decades consisted of the ability to survive with relatively small means on well-kept, micro-tourism establishments. Activity was characterised by continuity in a small but stable market with guests coming year after year. The market was small, i.e. narrow, but not in the geographical sense, because it comprised the whole country. This type of tourism developed under local conditions. A number of establishments existed.

Problems started surfacing when *generations* or owners changed. This often takes place during changes in market demand. Those taking over did so under different conditions. One was competence. Which aspects of the competence of their predecessors would be needed in order to survive in future? What more is needed? Or, in other words, what is the importance of earlier experiences for the next phase of tourism development in a peripheral area such as Tärnaby-Hemavan, and how can one take advantage of this? It should be mentioned here that, to a great extent, creativity is based on tradition. The transfer of knowledge is therefore of vital importance. All this depends on the effectiveness of the local network and networks covering large areas as well as the relationship between the local and the external.

The latter relationship here covers almost everything and can be expressed in the following question: how big will the sphere of action be for the local, small-scale enterprises in tourism and the other services, when external entrepreneurs have taken their share of the local arena? The development which has taken place since the end of the 1980s has mainly been directed by external actors. This is linked to the fact that the smaller tourism enterprises were left out of larger projects. This probably means that the development of tourism in future will also be directed by external forces. This need not be negative for the tourism industry, but the ability to maintain a distinctive local or regional profile will eventually decrease, as will the possibility of holding on to important actors. It is against this background that some people want to see the role of TPR strengthened in order to muster all the relevant actors in the local arena. This ambition has, nonetheless, met with opposition as the new constellations of actors do not necessarily see the local arena as the most important one.

This brief survey has described the development of the tourism industry over a period of 70 years during which it evolved from a local and, in some respects, a relatively closed arena, to an arena which is more open to influences and to forces in the national as well as the international market.

The developments in the Tärna region reflect changes that have taken place outside the locality – be they the general development of society, economic preconditions or something else – in the nation or at a supranational level. On the other hand, the locality offers enabling as well as constraining conditions. It is enabling in that it provides individuals with resources and knowledge on which they can act, both in the knowledge provided and in the milieus in which it can be used.

References

Åqvist, A.-C. (1992) Tidsgeografi i samspel med samhällsteori. *Meddelande från Lunds universitets geografiska institutioner* 115. Lund: Lund University Press.

Giddens, A. (1979) *Central Problems in Social Theory*. London: Cambridge University Press.

Törnqvist, G. (1986) *Svenskt Näringsliv ut Geografiskt Perspektiv*. Stockholm: Liber Forlag.

Chapter 8

Tourism's Role in New Rural Policy for Peripheral Areas: The Case of Arjeplog

PER ÅKE NILSSON

Ever since the EU (then the EEC) was formed in the 1950s, agriculture has been a major ingredient in its budget process. In 1992 the EU Common Agricultural Policy (CAP) was changed from promoting productivity increases to encouraging product development. Fewer subsidies and market orientation became the new policy. This forced less productive regions within the EU to diversify their agriculture. In 1996 the CAP was found to be successful and decisions were made to develop it further. One possible way of developing it was by forming a new policy for rural areas. This policy was based upon the comprehensive use of rural resources. An optimised use of local potential was suggested, resulting in a more balanced situation between traditional agriculture, other forms of rural activity and nature preservation interests. The aim was to help the farmer perform services more easily. The farmer would increasingly become a rural entrepreneur. Local identity, endogenous potential and understanding environmental protection became the keywords (SOU, 1996: 65).

One of the reasons behind the EU's interest in a new rural policy was a desire to halt the urbanisation wave that had swept over the Union since the 1950s, causing severe depopulation of certain rural areas. A new rural policy might give local residents the possibility of remaining in the countryside. It might also create or reinforce local identity, revealing endogenous potential necessary for peripheral development. Finally, a new rural policy can provide the basis for a local understanding of environmental protection, which is necessary for sustainable development, both locally and globally. This chapter examines the use of tourism as part of the new rural policy in the remote region of Arjeplog in northern Sweden. Following a general discussion of the policy and the issues it raises, it examines the particular problems of Arjeplog before focusing on a tourism project being implemented there.

Characteristics of the New Rural Policy

The new rural policy raises issues about relations between core and periphery, about production control and about the environment. First of all, however, it is necessary to understand that rural areas are not as homogeneous as we may think. We like to see them as places of tranquillity and contemplation, with traits of *backwardness* – from an urban viewpoint there is a different way of living and a different breed of locals there. City dwellers often regard the countryside as a free space with unlimited access. In Sweden *Allemansrätten* (the right of access for all) is often referred to. As the pressure for greater public access to recreational space in the countryside increases (thanks particularly to the emergence of a *recreational proletariat*), against a background of resistance from major landowners, a mixture of private ownership with open access systems like *Allemansrätten* may become appealing.

Allemansrätten

There are different opinions on the origin of *Allemansrätten* (Mortazavi, 1994) but historically it is evident that the vast forest areas in Sweden were not considered valuable by their owners before the timber period in the mid-19th century; until then they were used only for pasture, firewood or berry-picking. Indeed, the state forced locals to own the forest land in order to tax them as property owners. This is one reason why it was so easy for timber companies to buy the forest land for almost nothing during the last part of the 19th century. Thus the starting point for the emergence of *Allemansrätten* was the freedom from any regulation. Once established it was in the interest of the urban majority of the Scandinavian population to maintain this view of free access to the forest areas because of city dwellers' need for recreation.

Allemansrätten is no law despite its name, but a customary right relying on mutual respect. It offers everybody, regardless of citizenship:

- the right to cross property belonging to somebody else;
- the right to camp outdoors where ever you want and to stay overnight on a property belonging to somebody else;
- the use of waters owned by others for boating, bathing, cooking, etc.
- the right to pick wild flowers, berries and mushrooms anywhere.

There are, however, some restrictions:

- The privacy of the landowner must not be violated. The proper distance for passing or camping near a private house should be at least 20 m and it is desirable to keep out of sight.
- The economic interests of the landowners must not be disturbed and privately owned roads can be closed to motor vehicles.
- Endangered or protected species of wild flowers must not be picked.

With regard to the economic interests of the landowner, a recent verdict from the supreme court in Sweden ruled that it is acceptable to earn money by using somebody else's property. For a rafting company this is essential, since otherwise legal contracts with every landowner along a river, probably involving a fee, have to be made.

Rural Versus Urban

The longing for nature that is at the root of much conflict over land use today has existed for centuries and has many causes. Many urban people today embrace the Romantic view of the late 18th and 19th centuries whereby nature was seen as pure and good in opposition to the cultivated and civilised world. The image of the countryside as an incarnation of calm and reflection has for centuries been based on an idealised picture of the farmer, which ignores the grinding work involved. Even Marx, who portrayed farmers as backward people, described a mentally ideal state consisting of reading, writing, socialising with friends and the ability to 'dip the hook into the river' (Sörlin, 1993). Today, rural life is regarded as a form of recreation (Nilsson, 1995).

The French historian Braudel characterises Mediterranean man (*sic*) in the following manner: 'as a farmer by necessity but rural against his will, the Mediterranean man is living as an urban man' (Braudel, 1990). It may be possible to reverse the statement as follows: 'as an urban man by necessity but urban against his will, the Nordic man is living like a farmer' (Wiklund, 1993). Nordic people always look for the rural in their towns: parks, green areas, trees and bushes. According to the Romantic movement, being in nature is where man becomes a whole and noble human being, nature is a place of contemplation and inner development (Carlestam, 1994; Gustafsson, 1993). Many studies of tourism show that tourists seek wholeness in the different and that everyday life cannot offer this (MacCannell, 1992).

Uses, users and goals in the countryside

The problem for rural areas in northern Sweden seems to be that uses, users and goals do not fit in very well with each other. The uses in this study are of natural resources and include forestry, reindeer-herding, recreation and preservation of nature-based resources. The users of these nature-based resources are local residents, the tourism industry and conservationists. The latter want to protect the nature-based resources from their users but as – in many cases – they are representatives of the state and the common good, they are in favour of the use of these resources for recreation. Therefore national politicians have decided upon several goals, opening up the countryside for recreation by establishing *areas of national recreational interest*. This means that everybody in Sweden may have an interest in the use and development of these areas. This common interest in

Figure 8.1 Uses and users in presumed relation to each other

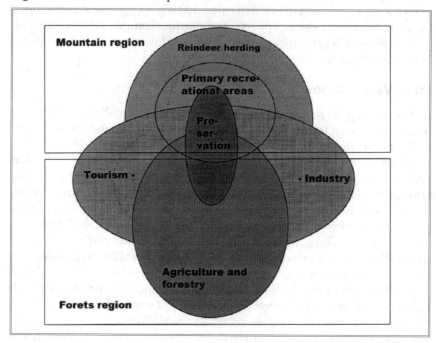

planning entitles the state to interfere with the community planning monopoly. Local politicians, on the other hand, often have a more pragmatic and locally biased view of how to use nature-based resources: they normally favour activities generating jobs. The relationship of uses and users in northern Sweden is shown in Figure 8.1.

Conflicts over uses, users and goals are compounded by the fact that the boundaries between rural and urban living are often blurred in northern Sweden. In the cities, many people maintain a rural lifestyle through rural tradition, land ownership in the countryside or through other ties with the countryside (Nilsson, 1996). On the other hand, there are many people living in the countryside who have an urban lifestyle. Many professions are urban in character and people may have personal grounds for maintaining an urban lifestyle.

This underpins the fact that the countryside is not homogeneous in the character of its social space. It consists of local residents with often contradictory interests and with different access to recreation facilities. Land ownership entitles access to most recreation activities. In Sweden lots of people in the countryside join different organisations which 'guard' their interests and function as lobby organisations. It is difficult to see how these organisations can reflect all the different interests and groups in the countryside.

Perspectives on Peripherality

Bearing in mind that rurality can be regarded as a form of peripherality, these differences may be further exacerbated by the different perspectives applied to the concept of peripherality.

Blomgren and Sørensen (1997) have noted a dichotomy between the concrete-practical perspective and the critical-reflexive perspective upon which the concept of peripherality is based in research (Blomgren-Jørgensen & Sørensen, 1997). By the concrete-practical perspective the authors mean a perspective which is based on factual information about the destination area. The critical-reflexive perspective takes the tourist-generating centres and their perceptions of peripherality/rurality as the point of departure, i.e. it views the destination from the eyes of the tourist. The authors find that, while these two perspectives often seem to be different, they are also interdependent.

The concrete-practical perspective gives the periphery attributes which are not necessarily inherent in the location but represent subjectively experienced symptoms of a periphery, e.g. traditional (old) architecture and unspoilt wilderness. These symbols of what tourists perceive as the attractiveness of the rural are exploited by urban tour operators, without any substantial consideration for the underlying reality.

The critical-reflexive perspective is based on ideas of rurality deeply rooted in mankind, but it ignores the actual reality existing in the countryside that gives rise to necessary change in order to sustain the rural community, the latter being the base for the interest of tourists in things rural. If the tourist is unable to see change in the countryside, he/she cannot see the ideas that are the basis for what is making the countryside attractive to him or her.

From the concrete-practical perspective, rural tourism conserves an image of the countryside which, according to the critical-reflexive perspective, can be an obstacle to its industrial development and also to the running of cultural heritage if it is not managed in a rational way. Tourism and regional development are issues that are dependent on each other: industrial development is the background which the rural lifestyle, promoted by the tour operators, must be projected upon in order to make it attractive. If there is no connection between the real modern lifestyle and the old lifestyle, the tourists will either see the old lifestyle as a non-existent and historical lifestyle and the whole countryside as a museum, or may feel cheated or annoyed by the discrepancy between what s/he has been promised and the not very exciting reality. For the Scandinavian mountain region, this is especially the case with the promotion of Saami culture,[1] in which Saamis are always dressed up in traditional costumes but appear in reality in 'normal' (western) clothes.

A new rural policy must be based on the interests of all actors in the rural area. Interests behind the different actors are often in line with each other but they may also cause problems. These problems must be identified step by step. The first step is to identify different uses and users and the second is to analyse the interests behind the identified users. The third step is to clarify what the conflicts of interest are and the problems raised by them. Finally, the results should be presented to politicians as a base for decision-making on a public choice basis.

Some research on preferences with regard to nature-based resources has been carried out. Koch and Søndergaard-Jensen (1988) have measured how forests in Denmark function as recreational areas. Lindberg and Johnson (1997) have written about local residents' attitudes to tourism. Public choice studies have been done in Sweden on nature as an externality (Mortazavi, 1995).

The following case-study raises questions about identity and provenance in the tourism industry as one of the users of nature-based resources in northern Sweden. The case is represented by a project on small-scale tourism enterprises in the communities of Arjeplog and Ammarnäs. The author has been familiar with these areas since 1965.

The Case of Arjeplog

Background

Arjeplog community is located in the county of Norrbotten and covers 13,000 km² (3% of Sweden's total area). In 1994 it had 3676 inhabitants (0.4% of the total population). The unemployment rate is 5.9% (1996). The community has no railway connection. A transborder highway – The Silver Road – runs through the community from Norway to the coast of the Bothnian Sea. The distance to the Atlantic coast at Bodø is 300 km. The distance to the Bothnian Sea (Skellefteå) is slightly more than 200 km and to Stockholm about 1000 km. The Arctic Circle crosses the northern part of the community, the location of which is shown in Figure 8.2. This mountain region has been falsely promoted as *Europe's last wilderness* (it is not, after all, untouched by human activity). Nevertheless a visit to the region is out of the ordinary and its natural resources offer great potential for tourism.

Ammarnäs is located in the community of Sorsele, at the end of a road heading west. It is considered to be in real wilderness. The village is small (250 inhabitants) but known for potato growing on a commonly owned hill – the potato hill – mostly because this is the only place where the climate allows people in Ammarnäs to cultivate potatoes. Perhaps this tradition has given the village an impetus to solve its problems collectively.

Arjeplog is by no means a homogeneous society. Its original inhabitants were the Saamis. Then came the settlers (hunters, fishermen and foresters), encouraged by a royal edict in 1751, some of whom subsequently became miners. Arjeplog's early economy was based on reindeer-herding and silver-mining (silver was discovered close to the Norwegian border in the 17th century and made the area locally famous – hence The Silver Road. It still has a well-visited Silver Museum). Merchants and craftsmen later

Figure 8.2 Northern Sweden and the communities of Arjeplog and Sorsele

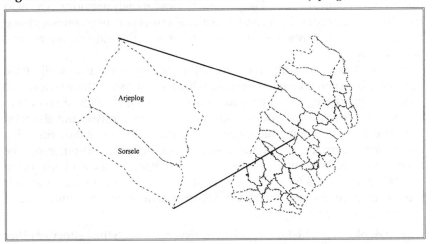

found their way to the municipal centre. In the middle of the 20th century, a lead mine was opened about 50 km from the centre. The population is hence a mix of traditionally macho miners, nature-bound settlers, people with an urban lifestyle in the municipal centre, and Saamis in the mountain range. The former two groups have cultivated a *hillbilly* lifestyle centred on hunting, fishing and snow-scooter riding, which is now under threat. The latter have often opposed attempts to encourage them to diversify into tourism, seeing these as interfering with their herding activities.

In the 1980s some German car testers came to Arjeplog and tried to make a test-driving track on the ice of the big lake Hornavan, just outside Arjeplog municipal centre. Local people helped them clear snow from the ice and a cooperative arrangement began: today this has resulted in 200 testers from all over the world gathering in Arjeplog every day from Christmas to Easter (the low season for the tourism industry).

At the beginning of the 1990s Boliden – the mining company which owned the Laisvall Lead Mine – announced that the mine would have to close in the near future. The politicians were panic-stricken and proposals were sent to government. The result was a grant of SEK100 million (£10 million) for social development after the closure of the mine. A committee was established to spread this money constructively and it managed to resist claims from the 3000 inhabitants that they should each get an equal share. After five years the committee had distributed the money and established many new jobs (NUTEK, 1996). Best of all, the mine is currently running better than ever!

The new jobs created by the grant were mainly in the public-service sector, though some were in the private-service sector. The miners did not consider these white collar jobs 'real' jobs. They despised them, but local women did not and have been showing less and less interest in the masculine hillbilly culture of yore. The prospects for averagely or poorly educated men have thus become bleak and the suicide rate is now high among young men in remote forest regions: to put it another way, there are too many guns and too few women.

A new dimension to the conflicts within society is clear: as well as the difference between miners, settlers, merchants and Saamis, there is now also a gender difference. It is often said that men are the losers in this context. Women are leaving the countryside for an urban lifestyle and the men remain in the backwoods surroundings. But the other side of the coin is that the women will probably find themselves sitting behind a computer in some megalopolis suburban environment for the rest of their lives, with no roots or natural context to fall into. The men are, if only by default, maintaining their fathers' cultural heritage and showing responsibility for the countryside.

To sum up the background:

- Arjeplog has a history not always congruent with the history of other parts of Sweden.
- The image of Arjeplog is silver, although it might as well have been lead.
- Arjeplog is a multi-ethnic society.
- One of the ethnic groups, the Saamis, are organised into three Saami villages with special views on how to use the recreational area within the mountain range.
- Another 'ethnic group', the settlers, has difficulties with its identity.
- A third group, the residents of the centre of Arjeplog with an urban lifestyle, cannot always cope with life in such a remote location over a whole lifecycle.
- The fourth group, the miners, has a rather conservative view of labour and the labour market.
- Within the municipal administration, a culture has been established allowing initiatives and ideas that are out of the ordinary.
- The car testers have given an impetus to local society, showing that exogenous influences can be of great value.

Taken together these things have probably created a culture where it was possible both to think of asking for SEK100 million as a grant and also to get it. And as an aftermath to the grant, a new tourism project involving eight entrepreneurs was started.

Tourism in Arjeplog

The tourism industry was already well established in Arjeplog before the project began, but its share of the market was poor (see Table 8.1). Wages also tended to be higher in other sectors, especially mining. Recreation is primarily devoted to fishing, hunting and mountain walking or

Table 8.1 Employment in Arjeplog by branch of industry, 1994

Industry	Share of total labour force (%)
Agriculture and forestry	6
Hotel and restaurant	7
Recreation and leisure	3
Leasing	2
Transport	7
Other private service	11
Manufacturing	13
Mining	15
Public service	28

trekking. Fishing rights are held by the owners of the waters but most of them have agreed upon the common use of lakes and rivers. Sport fishing in northern Sweden is focused on trout and char. Arjeplog has 8700 lakes and 3700 km of rivers, which probably makes it the most water-rich community in the world. Seventy percent of all tourists say they come for fishing (Slutrapport, 1996).

West of Odlingsgränsen (the border or limit for cultivation), fishing and hunting has been restricted to Saamis but several of the lakes located there have been opened to those with a licence. The state is the landowner in this region and the users are the reindeer-herders. The state is also a big land-owner east of Odlingsgränsen and there the land is managed by a state company, AssiDomän. The area available for hunting west of Odlingsgränsen in Arjeplog is 11,000 km². In 1990 there were 3000 day permits sold for hunting in this area. The optimal figure is estimated to be 15,000 day permits, although some researchers estimate it to be over 50,000 day permits for grouse. As a goal for visitors, in 1996 10,000 day permits were considered reasonable.

The trail system in the Swedish mountain region is highly developed. Kungsleden – The King's Trail – runs through Arjeplog from Abisko in the far north to Ammarnäs as the end station in the south. It has been unofficially extended to Dalarna. The famous part of the trail is, however, from Abisko to Kebnekaise, where huge numbers of ramblers pass. A substantial number also goes further south to Sarek. Sarek is one of the wildest parts of the Swedish wilderness, with free access for tourists but no facilities. Not very many people walk all the way down to Ammarnäs.

There is a capacity gap for hotels, holiday villages and youth hostels in the inland region. The rate of occupancy has decreased and is so low that summer peaks do not even reach 50% (Larsson, 1996). Numbers of second homes have expanded in Sweden from 200,000 in 1960 to 700,000 today.

The Project

This case study of Arjeplog is based on a project that started in the village of Ammarnäs and the community of Sorsele in 1995 (Projektplan, 1995). It is called 'New Methods for Production and Distribution of Nature-based Small-scale Tourism'. A development group within the community public sector launched the idea of giving some of the entrepreneurs in Arjeplog and Ammarnäs a chance to develop their communities both cooperatively and with professional help from outside. The quantitative objectives are a doubling of the turnover and the number of employees in the participating firms during the period. The time plan for the project is shown in Table 8.2. In order to make the firms cooperate, they were invited to invest labour and equipment for a certain sum of money. The same amount of money would then be contributed to the project by the Swedish Agency for Development of Commerce and Technology (NUTEK). The money was supposed to be used to invest in knowledge and networking.

The reason the public sector was willing to initiate and participate in this project may be the result of the community's five years of experience of handling the government grant of SEK100 million for development. There was already a milieu of development ideas in the community.

The project is based on rural tourism. Over the past few decades, rural tourism has become an increasingly important part of rural development strategies. Politicians at various levels have seen tourism as an instrument for modifying rural development and they are eager to form a new regional policy where local residents and tourism operators play a leading role to form development strategies. The question is whether tourism can function as a basis for such a policy, either by itself or with other actors.

Table 8.2 Timescale of activities planned for the project

Activity	Duration
Analysis of the situation today	1 Sept.-31 Dec. 1995
Market analysis	1 Sept.-31 Dec. 1995
Product development plan	1 Nov. 1995-30 June 1996
Market development plan	1 Nov. 1995-30 June 1996
Distribution plan	1 Nov. 1995-30 June 1996
Plan for competence development	1 Sept.-31 Dec. 1995
Product development	15 May 1996-1 Sept. 1997
Distribution development	15 May 1996-1 Sept. 1997
Marketing development	15 May 1996-1 Sept. 1997
Competence development	During the whole process
Local anchoring	During the whole process
Evaluation	1 Sept. 1997-31 Dec. 1998
Final documentation	1 June-31 Dec. 1998

At the time of writing the plan had not been properly followed because of the participants' views concerning the internal ranking of the activities. The whole project has been prolonged for two years and evaluation was to be finished by 1 July 2000. The final evaluation will be based on a report using the work done for this chapter as its base, and an independent economic evaluation which is taking place simultaneously. As a first step, this chapter looks at how far the firms operating a tourism business in Arjeplog are based on indigenous resources and how far they are relying on outside expertise. It assesses the relative merits of both approaches in creating a successful product.

The firms

The firms in the project can today offer high-quality ecotourism products but their products are fairly traditional and the demand for them is not sufficient for a decent turnover. Some of the firms are newly established but some have over 50 years of experience. The firms are presented in Table 8.3. Some form of ecotourism is expected to form the basis of the project. A lot has been written about ecotourism in general but the problem the firms were faced with was how to tackle the theories in practice and to discover the limits of ecotourism.

Table 8.3 The firms taking part in the project and their products

Firm	Product
Adolfströms Handelsbod & Stugby	Holiday village with local guide, traditional countryside shop, conferences
Arctic Life	Hunting packages and courses
Arjeplogs Hundspannresor	Dog sled tours and wildlife tourism
Båtsuoj	Sharing of Saami everyday life activities
Lapplandssafari	Package tours with hunting, fishing, Saami culture, guided tours, local meals
Vildmarkskonsulten	Package tours and activities
Vindelåforsens stugby	Holiday village
Vuoggatjålme	Holiday village, guided tours, conference, helicopter and aeroplane tours

The firms have agreed upon the following guidelines:

- to plan purchases according to the best environmental supply – if it is possible and rational, they buy locally;
- to try to minimise garbage;
- to try to minimise energy use;
- to jointly accept ethical codes which our customers are informed of on their arrival;

- to demand from suppliers environmentally sound products;
- to ask customers to participate in the development of products.

Social, cultural and ideological implications

The firms reflect the social reality existing in Arjeplog. Some of the firms are tied to Saami culture (Båtsuoj and Lapplandssafari). Others have their origin in the settler culture (Adolfströms Handelsbod & Stugby and Vindelåforsens Stugby). One reflects the urban–rural environment in central Arjeplog (Vildmarkskonsulten). Three use nature as the total basis for their existence (Vuoggatjålme, Arctic Life and Arjeplogs Hundspannsresor).

Because of the broad spectrum of Arjeplog society, the firms have great difficulty communicating or cooperating with each other. On the other hand, they have a great opportunity to offer something in common that is of a comprehensive nature with regard to tourist interests. They can also learn a lot from each other. The mix of social contexts in Arjeplog, together with the special natural conditions ('Europe's last wilderness'), constitutes a real competitive situation for the firms.

Environmental implications

Using the environment is the basic idea common to all the firms and it appears from their guidelines that, while conscious of global environmental problems and the need for sustainability, they are adopting a conservative approach respectful of existing social arrangements rather than seeking radical political change.

According to the guidelines to which the firms have agreed, they promise to buy locally if it is possible and to present ethical codes for their customers upon arrival, and to ask them to participate in their product development. The remainder are just a promise to try to reduce energy use and minimise garbage. It is obvious they do not intend to create radical changes in the environment. They all have problems with access to their activities: they are all at least 100 km from the airport, there is use of coaches, cars and helicopters. There are plastic boats. But the intention is to reduce and not increase the damage to the environment caused by their activities.

To conclude: the common feature is the environment but this is not the most creative or unique feature of the activities.

Regional development implications

The firms have a developmental approach. They want to be recognised as local enterprises and their products to be locally anchored. This is close to what a new rural policy should be about: designating local identity, revealing the endogenous potential necessary for development on the periphery.

Theories on regional development vary from a naive belief in spin-off effects from core regions to peripheral regions (Myrdal, 1957) to opinions that the dominance of the core will result in a brain drain and net capital flow from the periphery to the core (Stöhr, 1981). Today, the two ends seem to meet in a mixed theory showing that both core and periphery can be beneficial to each other (Brox, 1969; Ekman, 1991; Nilsson, 1991; Ronnby, 1994). Researchers who focus on the periphery have often seen local initiatives as the only way of development (Brox, 1969; Ekman, 1991; Nilsson, 1991; Ronnby, 1994). Local control and local anchoring is regarded as an important issue for the firms (de Kadt, 1979; Lickorish *et al.*, 1991; Nilsson, 1996). Sparsely populated areas in the periphery have a double problem: distance from the market and lack of infrastructure for service functions for residents. In Norway, some research has been done on the situation for people in such regions where the population is sparse and decreasing over the long term (Aasbrenn, 1995).

Some questions may be raised with regard to these research results: are the firms a product of exogenous processes, directed from the core or outside the region, or are they are a product of endogenous processes, arising within Arjeplog and Ammarnäs, based on local knowledge and tradition? Are the products of the firms locally anchored (Brox, 1969; Ekman, 1991; Henry & Kristensen, 1996)?

If placed on a continuum between a strictly endogenous origin and a strictly exogenous origin, the firms are clustered as in Figure 8.3. The firms' origins are now discussed more fully.

(1) Adolfström was started by a woman from Stockholm who moved to Adolfström, marrying one of five brothers in the village. The village was recognised to have no future but all the brothers married women from the south of Sweden and brought them to the village. Together, the women started many activities, such as a restaurant in the middle of nowhere – with car testers as customers in the winter and tourists in summer – an air service, and so on. The village is situated 100 km from Arjeplog down a no-through road. The Stockholm wives' experience was mixed with local tradition and culture. Local handicrafts are not sold in the shop, which sells things from all over Sweden. The product is hence both exogenous and endogenous.

(2) Arctic Life was started by a person from another part of northern Sweden, working within the Swedish Customs Agency. His product – hunting – is endogenous to the region and he has to cooperate with local landowners in order to perform his activity. This endogenous product is mixed, as it is run by a person of exogenous origin, having experience in a field quite different from tourism and private entrepreneurship. The owner's roots are, however, in the same type of society as Arjeplog.

(3) Hundspannsresor is run by a Norwegian couple with experience of running tours in Norway. They settled in a small village 40 km south of Arjeplog, in the middle of nowhere, because it was a suitable loca-

tion for dog-sled tours. Dog-sledding is not a local tradition and the couple do not have many customers from the community or the region. Their customers are mostly Germans. In order to maintain their business, they must both be friends with the landowners and use them for tracking and track maintenance. They also use them as guides. This is a typical exogenous product run in a context which fits in well with local traditions.

(4) Båtsuoj is run by a local Saami woman in a village not far from Arjeplog, and the product is highly local and thus endogenous. She cooperates closely with the local municipality and the schoolchildren of Arjeplog are sent to her camp for week-long field trips.

(5) Lapplandssafari is also run by a Saami woman, born in Ammarnäs. But she has been outside her home village for many years, living in Stockholm and active in the tourism industry (package tours). Her knowledge of Saami culture was rudimentary when she came back, although she has always been a member of the Saami village where she was born. The product is exogenous by its nature as a package tour operator, but is endogenous in the activities it offers and in the origin of the owner.

(6) Vildmarkskonsulten was started by a woman from Arjeplog, who had lived for a long time in Stockholm. She was employed by a tour operator, selling package tours to the north of Sweden. She left Stockholm and went back to Arjeplog with her project idea and is now running it from the destination instead of from the market. Her husband has experience of air traffic control. He is now offering tourists plane tours into the wilderness. The only endogenous part of the company is the origin of the owners and some parts of their activities. The business idea was stimulated by exogenous experiences.

(7) Vindelåforsen was started by the son of the owner of a holiday village in Ammarnäs. After academic studies in Umeå, specialising in pedagogy, he moved back to his roots together with his wife, an artist from the south of Sweden with experience of mental health training courses. The product is totally dependent on the owners' own experiences, knowledge and personalities. They sell themselves and not the local culture. But the man's local roots contribute to the product.

(8) Vuoggatjålme was started by the owner's mother, who was born in the south of Sweden and came to the mountain area of Arjeplog in the 1920s, where she started a mountain refuge for trekkers. The state owns the land and it is located within the territory of the Saami people. The owner has had very good relations with the Saami population but all the same is not allowed to own the land on which his house and home is located. The product is not typical for local people since it is based on trekkers and mountain lovers from the south of Sweden. But many local activities are also offered, like hunting and fishing. The owner is obviously a local person since he was born there.

Figure 8.3 Position of each firm on the continuum of endogenous and exogenous processes

Endogenous --(8)(4)----(5)-------(1)-(2)----(6)--(7)----(3)--   Exogenous processes   processes

The positions on the continuum are an estimate but the criteria are clear: origin of owners, origin of business idea, local anchoring of business activities. The results of this estimate of what is endogenous and what is exogenous show that there are wide differences among the firms. Some are owned and run by people who have never left Arjeplog, while others have been started by people from outside. But the products also differ, from having a pure local cultural context to being an *imported* product. Some products are mixtures of the endogenous and the exogenous. It is difficult to say anything about the value of exogenous or endogenous traits from this result. Any analysis must be combined with information on the way the firms act in the market.

Local production control

Production control within tourism has much to do with supply-oriented tourism versus demand-oriented tourism (Aasbrenn, 1995; Slee *et al.*, 1996; Westerdahl & Westlund, 1996). Demand-oriented tourism is dominated by the market. The tourist decides to go to a destination to satisfy her curiosity or is stimulated by marketing efforts. Supply-oriented tourism is dominated by the destination and the attraction. It can either be tourism offered by a supplier with almost no marketing effort or by suppliers with a good contact with tour operators in the market.

Northern Scandinavian tourism is predominantly supply-oriented, with some major exceptions, like Jukkasjärvi, Åre and Sälen in Sweden. The promotion of northern Sweden and Finland as the last wilderness of Europe within the EU, together with a yearly 5% increase in tourism in Europe, may change the conditions from supply-oriented tourism to demand-oriented tourism. In such a situation the local residents' trade-off propensity may be high, i.e. they may be willing to accept environmental and social disturbance for a better financial income from tourists. Local residents cannot be seen as a homogeneous group under such conditions: some gain from tourists, others find their lifestyle threatened, while others are not affected by any of these matters (Lindberg & Johnson, 1996; Nilsson, 1996).

A model of demand and supply for tourism is shown in Figure 8.4. DD stands for demand-oriented demand, i.e. the tourist has preferences without being exposed to any marketing effort. DS stands for supply-oriented demand, i.e. when the tourist makes perferences after being subjected to marketing efforts. SD stands for supply-oriented supply,

Figure 8.4 Supply and demand for tourism: a model

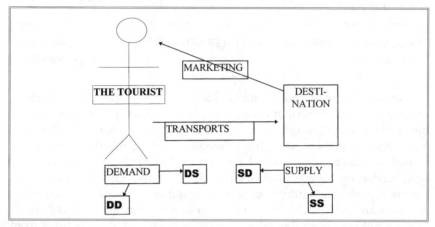

i.e. when the producer offers a product without contact with any form of market. DS and SD together stand for tourism that can be of substantial volume and tourism controlled by the operators in the market. They may be controlled by the producer if the attraction is a mega-attraction. When there is a supply-oriented supply (SS), the producer has full control over the situation but there will probably not be much to control.

Northern Scandinavia offers predominantly SS tourism. It is sometimes promoted by communities eager to put themselves on the map, but it is also promoted by people wanting to give tourists the same experiences that they find interesting themselves. If they find these experiences marvellous, then the tourists are expected to find them marvellous too. There are some exceptions to this rule, for instance Jukkasjärvi in Kiruna.

Globalisation versus localisation is another issue that affects the companies being studied, with communications, economy and culture as the main targets for globalisation, while politics, military strategies and citizenship are still issues of local or regional concern (Galtung, 1996). Placed on a scale of supply-orientation to demand-orientation, the companies will cluster as in Figure 8.5.

Figure 8.5 Position of each firm on the continuum of supply-orientation and demand-orientation

Localisation -----(8)-(4)-(1)-(5)-(2)---(3)-(7)(6)-------------Globalisation

(1) Adolfström is an SS product. It is based upon what is thought suitable to show the tourists. The company also runs a shop and local products are not sold to any great extent. On the contrary, most products come from outside. A dispute over pricing excludes much local handicraft.

(2) Arctic Life is an SD product. The product is controlled by the owners

but is adapted to a market and what the market wants. The owners have experience of this market and have brought their knowledge into the company.

(3) Hundspannsresor is an SD product. The owners have experience of the market and they actively target the German market. By using tour operators in Germany, Hundspannresor is similar to a DS product. It is well anchored among the local residents, including the Saami population.

(4) Båtsuoj is an SS product: the product is so attractive that there is no need for marketing.

(5) Lapplandssafari is an SS product because of its deep roots in the Saami culture.

(6) Vildmarkskonsulten is a typical SD product. It is focused on the demand side and has the experience to do this. It is very close to a DS product.

(7) Vindelåforsen is an SS product inasmuch as it will not give the customer anything the owners themselves do not want to offer. On the other hand, they recruit their customers by channels similar to those in a DS concept. Those coming know what to expect and they have consciously, and sometimes desperately, looked for the product.

(8) Vuoggatjålme is an SS product because of its deep roots in the settler culture. The product is also anchored in the Saami population.

Thus four of the companies are on the SS side, three are in the SD sphere and one has almost entered the DS sphere. The SD companies, close to becoming DS companies, are all exogenous, while the purely SS companies are highly endogenous. Most of the companies are careful to anchor their products among the local residents. If the firms' positions on the exogenous–endogenous continuum and the supply–demand continuum are compared, a pattern emerges. Hundspannsresor, Vildmarkskonsulten and Vindelåforsen have exogenous dimensions and are DS-type firms. Båtsuoj and Vuoggatjålme are endogenous in character and are also fairly SS-oriented. We can conclude from this that exogenous impact is necessary if people set up a business idea that is a target for competition. Båtsuoj and Vuoggatjålme have a nature and culture-based context which sells by itself to a certain extent; however, the lack of market orientation is probably also the result of the endogenous character of the owners.

Conclusions

The first part of this chapter focused on new rural policy. Such a policy should be based upon the comprehensive use of rural resources. An optimised use of local potential was suggested, resulting in a more balanced situation between traditional agriculture, other forms of rural activity and nature preservation interests.

The eight firms examined as part of an ongoing case study are anchored in the mixed context of Arjeplog: the Saami culture, the settler culture and the urban –rural culture of central Arjeplog. Because of their mixed origins, a comprehensive range of rural resources has indeed been used. The mix of endogenous and exogenous characteristics of both the persons involved and the products offered may be seen as a use of local potential, even if it is far from optimal. Together these conditions have the potential to develop a more balanced situation in Arjeplog between traditional industry (agriculture is non-existent) and other forms of rural activities, since the firms offer other forms of rural activities.

Preservation interests have been taken care of as far as the Local Agenda 21 dictates. No fundamental change in environmental policy has been achieved by the firms but this has obviously not been the intention. Making an effort within the system has been goal enough.

The major goal of the project has been the doubling of the number of persons employed within the firms. The possibility of achieving this goal is high and, by doing so, the firms give both themselves and the same number of other people the possibility of remaining in the region.

What is striking is the importance of exogenous impetus in the development activities. The development environment at the community office, together with the phenomenon of the car testers bringing exogenous elements into the everyday life of Arjeplog, have probably formed an acceptance of the exogenous ideas and inputs which are necessary for starting most of the firms.

The question of how to cope with the emergence of a *recreational proletariat* claiming the vast recreation areas of Arjeplog will not be settled by this project but it may indicate a way to cope with it. Almost all the firms have concrete experience of coping with local landowners or local users like the Saamis. On the other hand, they are not dealing with mass tourism; the bulk of the recreation proletariat is bound to use nationwide organisations for hunting or other forms of recreation. For these organisations, the interests of their customers will be more powerful than the interests of local residents. A mapping of different interests with regard to uses and users is necessary in order to clarify where compromises have to be reached before conflict between the interests breaks out. If the state does not decide who has the right of access to recreation havens in the mountain region, the different interests will have to negotiate. Otherwise, the strongest – the recreation proletariat – will win.

Note

1. The word Saami is used throughout this chapter instead of the more internationally known Lap. Lap is Finnish and means wild-man. The Saamis themselves prefer to be called Saamis, which is officially respected in Sweden.

References

Aasbrenn, K. (1995) Livskraftige uttynningssamfunn. *NordREFO* 3.

Arjeplogsgruppen (1996) Slutrapport. *Samordningsgruppen för regionala utvecklingsinsatser i Arjeplog 1991 –1996*.

Blomgren-Jørgensen, K. and Sørensen, A. (1997) *Peripheral and Quaint: Reflections on Peripherality in Tourism Research*. Nexø: Research Centre of Bornholm.

Braudel, F. (1990) *Medelhavet – Rummet och Historien*. Stockholm: Gidlund.

Brox, O. (1969) *Nordnorgeplanen och Centralbyråkraterna*. Stockholm.

Carlestam, G. (1994) Framstegstanken kris. In I. Söderbaum (ed.) *Plats för Känsla*. Stockholm: National Council for Building and Research.

de Kadt, E. (ed.) (1979) *Tourism – Passport to Development?* Oxford: Oxford University Press.

Ekman, A.-K. (1991) Bottom-up strategies in theory and practice. *NordREFO* 4.

Galtung, J. (1996) *Peace by Peaceful Means: Peace and Conflict, Development and Civilization*. London: Sage.

Gustafsson, G. (1993) *Landscape, the Individual and Society*. Karlstadt: University of Karlstad.

Henry, M. and Kristensen, K. (1996) Economic Growth in Functional Regions. Paper presented in Washington, DC.

Koch, N.E. and Søndergaard-Jensen, F. (1988) *Skovenes Friluftsfunktion i Danmark – Forest Recreation in Denmark, Part IV*. København: Institut for Skov og Landskab.

Larsson, M. (1996) *Resandet till Fjällregionen*. Östersund: Arbetsmaterial Institutionen för turistvetenskap, Mitthögskolan.

Lickorish, L.J., Jefferson, A., Bodlender, J. and Jenkins, C. L. (1991) *Developing Tourism Destinations: Policy and Perspectives*. Harlow: Longman.

Lindberg, K. and Johnson, R. L. (1997) Modeling resident attitudes towards tourism. *Annals of Tourism Research* 24, 402–24.

MacCannell, D. (1992) *Empty Meeting Grounds*. London: Routledge.

Mortazavi, R. (1995) Three papers on the economics of recreation, tourism and property rights. *Umeå Economic Studies* 396, University of Umeå.

Myrdal, G. (1957) *Economic Theory and Undeveloped Regions*. London.

Nilsson, J.E. (1995) *Industrialiseringen i Sverige*. Stockholm.

Nilsson, P.Ä. (1991) *A Contribution to a New Type of Regional Policy*. Zagreb: Razvoj Development.

Nilsson, P.Ä. (1996) Local will and urban demand. Paper presented at the 4th Nordic Tourism Research Conference in Rovaniemi, December.

NUTEK (1996) Problem i gränslandet, Utvärdering av Arjeplogsgruppen. Stockholm: Närings och tecknikutrecklingsverket, Swedish National Board for Industrial and Technical Development.

Projektplan (1995) Nya metoder för produktion och distribution av naturbaserad småskalig turism. Arjeplogs Utvecklingscentrum, Arjeplogsgruppen.

Ronnby, A. (1994) *Mobilising Local Communities* (p. 77). Mid-Sweden University.

Slee, R.W., Farr, H. and Snowden, P. (1996) *The Economic Impact of Alternative Types of Rural Tourism*. Aberdeen: Department of Agriculture, University of Aberdeen.

SOU (1996) *Administration av EU:s jordbrukspolitik i Sverige*. Stockholm.

Stöhr, W. (1981) *Development from Above or Below?* Vienna.

Sörlin, S. (1993) Bonden som ideal. In B. Larsson (ed.) *Bonden i Dikt och Verklighet*. Stockholm: Nordiska Museet.

Westerdahl, S. and Westlund, H. (1996) Sociala ekonomins bidrag till ny sysselsättning. Paper presented at seminar on regional research, Östersund, 13–14 November.

Wiklund, T. (1993) *Asatro och Träddyrkan – Nordiskt Perspektiv på Staden, Nordplan* (p. 7). Stockholm: Meddelande.

Index